Do it

alpha books

1. Learn only the present tense of the verbs you study. It usually is the only tense you need to know.

2. Always begin a request for help with a polite address such as "*Pardon.*"

3. Rent French movies with subtitles. This is the easiest way to learn pronunciation.

4. Make flash cards for yourself of useful vocabulary words. You can use these on the bus or the subway, while you wait for an appointment, or anytime you have a free moment.

5. Eat in French restaurants and read French cookbooks before your trip. You'll be able to figure out what you like and how to say it before you are in the hot seat.

alpha books

One luxurious
bubble bath

alpha books

A gourmet meal with a bottle of wine
(recruit a spouse or friend).

alpha books

License to sleep until noon
one weekend day.

alpha books

Time to recline and listen to a favorite CD
(preferably French).

cut

6. Read the instruction labels on new appliances and cosmetics. They often are written in both French and English. Compare the two to pick up new words.

7. When words fail, use your hands. There are many ways of pointing to communicate your needs and desires.

8. Before making a phone call in which you might need to speak French, write down a few key words and phrases that might come up so you'll be prepared.

9. Use cognates when you can. Many words are the same in French and English. They are just pronounced with a different accent.

10. Relax and maybe have a glass of wine when you talk or prepare to learn. Being calm and open makes learning and speaking French fun and much easier.

C O U P O N

C O U P O N

C O U P O N

C O U P O N

Learn
French

Learn French

Christophe Desmaison

The Lazy Way™

Macmillan • USA

Macmillan Publishing books may be purchased for business or sales promotional use. For information please write: Special Markets Department, Macmillan Publishing USA, 1633 Broadway, New York, NY 10019.

International Standard Book Number: 0-02-863011-4
Library of Congress Catalog Card Number 98-89560

01 00 99   8 7 6 5 4 3 2 1

Interpretation of the printing code: the rightmost number of the first series of numbers is the year of the book's printing; the rightmost number of the second series of numbers is the number of the book's printing. For example, a printing code of 99-1 shows that the first printing occurred in 1999.

Printed in the United States of America

Book Design: Madhouse Studios

Page Creation: Eric Brinkman

You Don't Have to Feel Guilty Anymore!

IT'S O.K. TO DO IT *THE LAZY WAY*!

It seems every time we turn around, we're given more responsibility, more information to absorb, more places we need to go, and more numbers, dates, and names to remember. Both our bodies and our minds are already on overload. And we know what happens next—cleaning the house, balancing the checkbook, and cooking dinner get put off until "tomorrow" and eventually fall by the wayside.

So let's be frank—we're all starting to feel a bit guilty about the dirty laundry, stacks of ATM slips, and Chinese takeout. Just thinking about tackling those terrible tasks makes you exhausted, right? If only there were an easy, effortless way to get this stuff done! (And done right!)

There is—*The Lazy Way*! By providing the pain-free way to do something—including tons of shortcuts and timesaving tips, as well as lists of all the stuff you'll ever need to get it done efficiently—*The Lazy Way* series cuts through all of the time-wasting thought processes and laborious exercises. You'll discover the secrets of those who have figured out *The Lazy Way*. You'll get things done in half the time it takes the average person—and then you will sit back and smugly consider those poor suckers who haven't discovered *The Lazy Way* yet. With *The Lazy Way,* you'll learn how to put in minimal effort and get maximum results so you can devote your attention and energy to the pleasures in life!

THE LAZY WAY PROMISE

Everyone on *The Lazy Way* staff promises that, if you adopt *The Lazy Way* philosophy, you'll never break a sweat, you'll barely lift a finger, you won't put strain on your brain, and you'll have plenty of time to put up your feet. We guarantee you will find that these activities are no longer hardships, since you're doing them *The Lazy Way*. We also firmly support taking breaks and encourage rewarding yourself (we even offer our suggestions in each book!). With *The Lazy Way*, the only thing you'll be overwhelmed by is all of your newfound free time!

THE LAZY WAY SPECIAL FEATURES

Every book in our series features the following sidebars in the margins, all designed to save you time and aggravation down the road.

- **"Quick 'n' Painless"**—shortcuts that get the job done fast.
- **"You'll Thank Yourself Later"**—advice that saves time down the road.
- **"A Complete Waste of Time"**—warnings that spare countless headaches and squandered hours.
- **"If You're So Inclined"**—optional tips for moments of inspired added effort.
- **"The Lazy Way"**—rewards to make the task more pleasurable.

If you've either decided to give up altogether or have taken a strong interest in the subject, you'll find information on hiring outside help with "How to Get Someone Else to Do It" as well as further reading recommendations in "If You Really Want More, Read These." In addition, there's an only-what-you-need-to-know glossary of terms and product names ("If You Don't Know What It Means, Look Here") as well as "It's Time for Your Reward"—fun and relaxing ways to treat yourself for a job well done.

With *The Lazy Way* series, you'll find that getting the job done has never been so painless!

Series Editor
Amy Gordon

Cover Designer
Michael Freeland

Editorial Director
Gary Krebs

Managing Editor
Robert Shuman

Development Editor
Alexander Goldman

Director of Creative Services
Michele Laseau

Production Editor
Scott Barnes

What's in This Book

Introduction

Congratulations! If you've just picked up this book, you are on your way to learning French the easiest way possible—*The Lazy Way*. *Learn French The Lazy Way* proves that you don't need to spend a year abroad or enroll in time-consuming, expensive classes to pick up the basics of the language. Unlike other books about learning French—phrase books, which deal exclusively with situation-based problems, and textbooks, which are dry, comprehensive, and filled with every nuance of verb conjugation—*Learn French the Lazy Way* offers helpful shortcuts, clever strategies, and fun exercises that make learning French simple, enjoyable, and most importantly, stress-free. Best of all, the 12 lessons and many more tips you'll find here can be approached methodically as a program or can be taken at your whim, *a la carte*.

I know all about learning a language *The Lazy Way* because I've helped many of my friends do it. Take my girlfriend, for example. Although she took French classes throughout high school and even into college (seven years worth!), she found to her *horreur* the first time she visited France that most of what she learned had not stuck and what had stuck was not relevant to her life. (Turns out you rarely need to say "chalkboard" outside of a classroom.) She was disheartened but determined to become fluent. She tried everything. She enrolled in more expensive classes. She tried to read novels with a dictionary by her side but to no avail. Then she found something that really motivated her—a French boyfriend. I made her realize that she was trying too hard. Instead of learning every word of French she could, she needed to focus on learning just the ones that matter. When she adopted my lazy method, it worked. She no longer lamented that she had forgotten the word for "wrought-iron", which she'd never need to use, or that she couldn't remember three synonyms for "to go" when one works fine. Now when she visits France, she can order food with confidence, can read signs in museums, can buy clothing, can take public transportation, and can even enjoy pleasant conversations with natives like my family and friends. *Vive le Lazy Way!*

This book is organized according to what you really need to know. It starts with the tools and resources that are most handy, a simple pronunciation reference, as well as other types of books you might want to refer to as you learn. After that, it conquers French in order of importance: cognates, nouns, adjectives, and verbs. There are also handy chapters on how to be extremely polite to get what you want as well as ones on the really fun stuff like shopping, dining, traveling, chatting, and so on.

This book is not a complete French course—happily so. Most foreign-language books devote pages upon pages to mysteriously labeled parts of speech that most of us can't even identify in English. In my opinion, if you speak English successfully without knowing off the top of your head what direct-object pronouns and past-perfect verb tenses are, you'll be just fine learning French without knowing them, too. If you really want to learn to say things like "I had hoped you would have understood me," you should probably sign up for expensive immersion classes after all. This book teaches you to identify some of the more sophisticated constructions you might hear but focuses on keeping things simple.

The most important lesson in this book is that learning and using French should be a pleasurable experience. This book contains no tests and no grades (thank heavens!), and you should work at your own pace. Do not press yourself to become fluent overnight. It takes years of constant practice and study to do so. What *can* be accomplished *The Lazy Way* is building a working knowledge of the language and the tools you need to converse in it. *Learn French The Lazy Way* will give you all you need to know to start enjoying the pleasures of a country with a beautiful language and a rich history.

Acknowledgments

Thanks to all the people who helped me on this book: Susannah and Jennifer Griffin, Sharon Bowers, and Gabrielle Euvino; Lydia Wills, my agent; Amy Gordon, acquiring editor and founder of *The Lazy Way* series; and Alex Goldman, a talented and very patient line editor.

Vive la Différence!
French at a Glance

Are you too lazy to read *Vive la Différence!* French at a Glance?

1 You haven't reached Chapter 1 yet, and you already are overwhelmed. ☐ yes ☐ no

2 You think French is as difficult to learn as Russian, and you suspect they use the same alphabet. ☐ yes ☐ no

3 You are surprised to learn that French numbers are pronounced differently. After all, they look exactly the same. ☐ yes ☐ no

Stranger in a Strange Language: What You Should Know Before We Start

French is a romance language as well as a romantic language. Romance languages are based on Latin and resemble other romance languages such as Spanish and Italian. Although English is not a romance language, you will be pleasantly surprised to see that your knowledge of English will make learning French a breeze.

DO YOU SPEAK ANY OTHER LANGUAGES?

If you already speak or are familiar with another language—especially a romance language—French will be even easier to learn. Having another language under your belt builds confidence. It makes you realize that you can teach an old (or lazy) dog new tricks. Most European languages share similarities.

Sometimes elements you remember from one language can be appropriated to help you learn or at least get by in another language.

Did you ever learn Latin or Greek? Although Latin and ancient Greek no longer are spoken, they are the basis of most European languages. Many roots of words in English, German, French, Italian, and Spanish date back to these two languages. Look at a word you don't know and see if there is anything familiar about it. What is the root? If you can get to the root, you can figure out the essence of the word's meaning. Say the root aloud and then say other words that remind you of it. You just might be able to match up a meaning.

I am not going to recommend that you extensively conjugate verbs; that's not *The Lazy Way* of doing things. Just to show you how similar French is to other romance languages, however, look at the following verb conjugations to see how alike they are.

French

je (I)	suis
tu (you, singular)	es
il/elle (he/she, singular)	est
nous (we)	sommes
vous (you, plural)	êtes
ils/elles (they)	sont

Italian

io	sono
tu	sei
lei	è
noi	siamo
voi	siete
loro	sono

Spanish

yo	soy
tú	eres
usted	es
nosotros	somos
vosotros	sois
ustedes	son

Many of the words in one language often translate into similar words in another language. Take the word "sun," for example. In French, it is *soleil*; in Italian, it is *sole*; in Spanish, it is *sol*. There are countless other examples like this one, such as the verb "to repeat." In French, it's *répéter*; in Italian, it's *ripetere*; in Spanish, it's *repetir*.

One particularly fun example of similarities occurs in the days of the week and the months, many of which are named for ancient gods, goddesses, and emperors.

IF YOU'RE SO INCLINED

Note that English days primarily are named for the Norse gods and goddesses, whereas those of the romance languages come from the Latin gods and goddesses.

English

Monday	The moon's day
Wednesday	Odin's day (Odin was a Norse god)
January	named for Janus
March	named for Mars
June	named for Juno
October	named for the Roman emperor Octavian

French

Lundi	The moon's day (*lune* is moon in French)
Mercredi	Mercury's day
Janvier	named for Janus
Mars	named for Mars
Juin	named for Juno
Octobre	named for the Roman emperor Octavian

Italian

Lunedi	The moon's day (Are you noticing a trend?)
Mercoledi	Mercury's day
Gennaio	named for Janus
Marzo	named for Mars

IF YOU'RE SO
INCLINED

Note that French and Italian are more similar to each other than either is to English.

Giugno	named for Juno
Ottobre	named for the Roman emperor Octavian

The bottom line is that most of the languages in the world are somehow related to others, and many of the words cross over. Those that don't can be explained by deeper examination. This book will not concern itself with deep examination or intricacies, but I hope this very brief word on language origins will make you realize that French is not as foreign or as inexplicable as you might have previously thought.

RELAX AND ENJOY

Having the right attitude is half the battle. When you are relaxed and laid back about learning and speaking French, you'll have an easier time. This is one of the terrible catch-22s of learning a foreign language because it usually is stressful to plunge into the unknown. Here are some tips:

- **Be humble.** Do not try for perfection. Your goal here should be to make yourself understood, not to be correct. Of course, it is wonderful to feel eloquent and graceful, but chances are you will be clunky and awkward starting out. Don't beat yourself up about it. Realize that you will make mistakes; it's part of how you learn. Babies fall down about as much as they stand up when they are learning to walk for the first time. You are in the same situation. The opposite also is true. If you're not making any mistakes, you probably aren't learning anything.

YOU'LL THANK YOURSELF LATER

Don't try to learn two languages at once. If you know another language better than you know French, it's only natural to confuse the two when you start learning French. Stay focused on French.

■ **Have a sense of humor.** Language mistakes can be very funny. The quirks and differences in a language are part of what makes learning it fun. Everyone returns from their first trip to France with a cute story of a terrible language blunder. Most of the time, everyone—including the French person who pointed out the mistake—had a good laugh about it.

■ **Do whatever you must to loosen up.** Do you drink? A glass of wine is a wonderful lubricant for conversation in any language. If you think you'll be involved in heavy conversation, consider preparing yourself with a nice, relaxing meal and a glass of wine first.

THE TOOLS OF THE TRADE

You really ought to have a few things in addition to this book to aid and abet your learning process. If you are serious about learning French, they will be of great use.

Buy a good dictionary. Make it small enough that it's not a chore to pick up but bigger than just a collection of phrases. A good paperback dictionary won't cost more than $15 and will last you many happy years. (It also will come in handy for crossword puzzles, which always seem to call for a word of French here or there.)

If you really are motivated and want to go the extra nine yards, you might want to buy some other books as well.

■ *A book of French verbs.* Several good collections of verbs outline all the conjugations you'll ever need. If you think you'll want to talk about all the fancy things you do, this is a good investment.

- *A book of French vocabulary words and/or phrases.* Many noun, phrase, and idiom books are fun and are good for more advanced study.

- *A French textbook.* If you like to do exercises, consider buying a French textbook. These books have chapters with progressively difficult lessons that serious students might like to own.

- *A little blank notebook.* Buy a small notebook and fill it with the words and phrases you want to learn so you can drill yourself at convenient times.

- *Index cards.* Learning French with a friend? Maybe you want to make flash cards and test one another. Write the French word on one side and the English translation on the other. Quiz one another when you feel like it.

OTHER WAYS TO LEARN

Books are great, but many of the best ways to enjoy French as you learn and to make the language really stick require you to leave the comfort of your own home. Try these ideas.

- **Join your local Alliance Française.** Many of these French culture centers are located around the U.S. They offer wonderful resources including lectures, movie series, classes, language labs, and libraries.

QUICK ⬤ PAINLESS

If you have a long train ride in the morning—that's a perfect time to study painlessly!

I've included a list of some of my favorite movies in Chapter 3 of this book.

■ **Find a study partner or a conversation group.** As with exercise, sometimes it's easier to motivate yourself if you have a trainer or a partner. There are many conversation groups in cities around the country. Your local Alliance Française might be able to match you up with a group of people at your ability level.

■ **Rent French movies.** France has a rich cinematic tradition. Movies bolster language skills, aid pronunciation, and give you insight into the culture.

■ **Read French newspapers or fashion magazines.** Like movies, newspapers are a window to the soul of a nation. Words you pick up in newspapers often are very useful, and they make you look impressively well-informed. French fashion magazines are similar to their American counterparts. Hence, you'll easily be able to discern the topics being discussed.

■ **Tune in to French television and radio.** Check your local listings to see whether any French programs are offered. In New York City, for example, there are many opportunities to see French news, French movies, and a popular talk show called *Bouillon de Culture* on the CUNY channel.

■ **Surf the World Wide Web.** Go online and see what you turn up. You'll find an astounding number of sites concerning French language, culture, and chats.

■ **Plan a trip to France.** There's no better way to learn a language than to be immersed in it. Granted, trial by fire can be scary, but you'll be surprised at how motivated you are to learn when the simple act of feeding yourself and getting around requires you to learn a bit of French.

- **Get a pen pal.** Being involved in someone else's life and activities is one of the most gratifying ways to learn French. You'll see what a real French person is up to day-to-day, and you'll make a new friend.

- **Host a foreign exchange student.** You'll certainly pick up some French if a French student stays at your house. When you visit France, you'll then have someone who can do the same for you.

ACTIVITY: THE NAME GAME

Here are the names of several famous French people. Using the letters in their names, can you create other French words?

> Example: Catherine Deneuve
> thé (tea), hier (yesterday), rien (nothing) venir (to come), veau (veal), dénier (to deny), dénué (devoid of), créer (to create) …

Gerard Depardieu

Jacques Cousteau

François Mitterand

Jules Verne

Guy de Maupassant

Claude Debussey

IF YOU'RE SO
INCLINED

Attend religious services in French if they are offered in your area. Catholic masses are composed of many listen-and-repeat segments, so going to church can become a little language lab.

Chapter two

Kid's Stuff: A-B-Cs and 1-2-3s

One of the easiest ways to look good is to perfect your pronunciation. If you have an ear for French, you'll be able to finesse your way through the language with aplomb. If you don't, no worries—the French generally find American accents charming.

Let's face it. Learning French pronunciation from a book is difficult. I've developed a new system, however, that I think is easier than the other ones I've seen (see the following list). The best way to learn to pronounce words correctly is to hear French being spoken. The laziest way to accomplish this is to rent French movies with subtitles. Subtitles can help you compare the words to the pronunciations. Be forewarned, however, that translations are rough and do not necessarily tell you the laziest way to say something. Still, watching French movies and hearing real French people speak certainly is the best—and most enjoyable—way to pick up the rhythm of the language.

YOUR A-B-Cs (AH-BAY-SAYs): PRONUNCIATION

French becomes much easier to speak when you know your A-B-Cs—or in this case, Ah-Bay-Says. The French alphabet is identical to the English alphabet; only the pronunciation is different.

Here is a list of the letters of the alphabet. Note that the pronunciation of some letters differs greatly from English, while the pronunciation of other letters is similar in French and English.

a	ah. As in what you say when the doctor tells you to stick out your tongue.
b	bay.
c	say.
d	day.
e	uh. This is what slipped out of your mouth in high school when the teacher called on you and you didn't know the answer. It's sort of a cross between eh and uh (close to euh).
f	f. Just like in English.
g	zsjay. Think of Zsa Zsa Gabor when you say this one. It is similar to jay but with a funkier beginning sound.
h	ah-sh. Like ash pronounced with a soft "a."
i	ee. Like leek.
j	zsee. Think of Zsa Zsa again on this one. This is similar to gee (as in "gee-whiz")

	but again with a funkier starting sound. Note that it's as if the English pronunciations of g and j are transposed.
k	kah. This is what people drive in the Boston area. Pahk the kah in Hahvahd Yahd.
l	l.
m	m.
n	n.
o	o.
p	pay.
q	coo. This is the sound doves make only more clipped.
r	air.
s	s.
t	tay.
u	oo. As in toot.
v	vay.
w	doob-leh vay. In English, we view "w" as a double "u." The French view it as a double (pronounced doob-leh) "v" (vay).
x	eeks. Like leeks.
y	ee-greck. Ee like leeks followed by greck, which sounds like the word children make when they think something is icky—bleck.
z	zed.

QUICK  PAINLESS

When you speak French, make sure you enunciate. No matter how exaggerated you think your accent sounds, it probably is still not strong enough. The stronger you make it, the more French you'll sound.

Accents

Five accents appear in French to indicate how a word should be pronounced.

- *Accent aigu:* The "e" at the end of words is not pronounced in French unless there's an accent aigu over it. *Passé* (out of style) is pronounced pahss-ay; *passe* (pass) is pronounced pahss. *Accent aigu* also can appear elsewhere in a word: *économie* is pronounced ay-conomee, whereas *elle* is pronounced with an eh sound (ehl) not an ay sound.

- *Accent grave:* Pronounced grahv. An example is *grève* (strike). An *accent grave* over an "e" means that the eh sound is even heavier. I think of *accent grave* as lending gravity to the "e."

- *Cédille:* This squiggly thing hangs off the bottom of a "c" to signify a soft sound. For example, *façade* is pronounced fa-sahd not fa-kayd.

- *Tréma:* A *tréma* (also called an umlaut in English) over an "i" indicates that the "i" should be pronounced separately. For example, *egoïste* is pronounced ay-go-east. Without the *tréma* over the "i," we'd be tempted to blend the "o" and the "i," making the word rhyme with moist.

- *Circumflex:* This hat-shaped accent is placed over vowels to indicate that their sounds should be shortened. For example, while it might take two seconds to say *cote*, it only takes one to say *côte*. The distinction is very subtle, so don't sweat it if you don't get it.

YOU'LL THANK YOURSELF LATER

When you see a circumflex and don't know what the word means, remember that it sometimes replaces an "s" (a relic from Old French). Add the "s" and see if you can figure out the word. For instance, *côte* means coast.

Silence is Golden

Many French letters are not pronounced, especially when they end a word:

Final e: *parle* (pahrl not pahr-leh or pahr-lay)

Final s: *compromis* (compro-mee not compro-meez)

H is never pronounced: *Helas* (ay-las) and *haute* (oat)

There are as many exceptions as there are rules in French pronunciation, especially where endings are concerned. Sometimes the letters are pronounced, as in *servir* (serv-ear); sometimes they are not, as in *parler* (par-lay). Again, your best bet in the pronunciation department is to watch French movies, speak to patient French people, and consult a dictionary or textbook when you run into trouble.

Easy as *Un-Deux-Trois:* Counting

One of the lazy ways to learn French is to gradually integrate it into your life—to let it infiltrate your English and really become your second language. To help you learn the French numbers, try counting the objects around you when you are on *le bus* or *le train*. Don't worry if you don't know the nouns. Just use the English nouns with a French accent.

un (une)	1	*six*	6
deux	2	*sept*	7
trois	3	*huit*	8
quatre	4	*neuf*	9
cinq	5	*dix*	10

The difference between *un* (the number one) and *une* (an article) is explained in Chapter 7, "You Say Potato, I Say *Pomme de Terre:* Nouns."

onze	11	*seize*	16
douze	12	*dix-sept*	17
treize	13	*dix-huit*	18
quatorze	14	*dix-neuf*	19
quinze	15	*vingt*	20

Higher Stakes

After you've mastered the basic numbers in the preceding list, raise the bar and count even higher. It's easier than it looks. *En effet* (in fact), the French are lazy themselves when counting above 50. They don't even bother to find new names for 70 and 90. They just add on. Pretty easy, *non?*

Note that the way French numbers higher than 10 are formed is quite different—and, I believe, easier to understand—from how they are formed in English.

Eleven through 16 are irregular, as in English. Then the numbers simply use 10 (or whatever prefix is added): 17 in French is expressed literally as 10-7, 18 as 10-8, and so on. When you hit 20, *vingt*, the pattern continues: 22 is expressed as 20-2, *vingt-deux*. The only difference is with the ones: 21, 31, and so on. These are expressed as 20 and 1, *vingt et un*, 30 and 1, *trente et un*, and so on.

After 69, things get even easier in French. The French way of expressing 70 is literally 60-10, *soixante-dix*. French for 71 is 60-11, *soixante-onze*. French for 72 is 60-12, 80 is 60-20, and so on.

Here are examples of the higher numbers.

zero	0	*soixante dix-neuf*	79
vingt et un (une)	21	*quatre-vingts*	80
vingt-deux	22	*quatre-vingt un (une)*	81
trente	30	*quatre-vingt-dix*	90
quarante	40	*quatre-vingt-onze*	91
cinquante	50	*cent*	100
soixante	60	*cent un*	101
soixante-dix	70	*deux cent*	200
soixante et onze	71	*deux cent un (une)*	201
soixante-douze	72	*mille*	1.000
soixante-treize	73	*un million*	1.000.000

Note that the French use periods in lieu of commas to separate the columns. Spaces also will work. If you want to make your numbers look even more impressively French, try drawing a visor on your ones (1) and a bar through your sevens (7).

Wow, you're really starting to fit in *en France.*

ACTIVITY: TONGUE TWISTERS AND CHILDREN'S VERSES

The French enjoy playing with language as much as we do. From a very early age, children are taught simple songs that they enjoy repeating. Even adults like tongue twisters. See if you can memorize some of these verses. That way you can repeat them to yourself—just as a French child would do—to reinforce your skills. Do not

IF YOU'RE SO
INCLINED

For any singers out there, try singing "99 Bottles of Beer on the Wall" with French numbers. The point is to have some fun with French numbers and to repeat them aloud many, many times.

worry about understanding the translations—many verses use coloquial words that are difficult to learn.

Tongue Twisters

Les chaussettes de l'archiduchesse sont sèches, archisèches.

The socks of the archduchess are dry, extra dry.

Panier cru, panier cuit, piano cru, piano cuit.

Raw basket, cooked basket, raw piano, cooked piano.

Children's Verses

Frère Jacques, Frère Jacques,
Dormez-vous? Dormez-vous?
Sonnez les matines, Sonnez les matines.
Ding, ding, dong. Ding, ding, dong.

Brother James, Brother James,
Are you sleeping? Are you sleeping?
Ring the morning bells. Ring the morning bells.
Ding, ding, dong. Ding, ding, dong.

Fais dodo, Colas, mon petit frère
Fais dodo, t'auras du lolo
Maman est en haut, qui fait un gâteau
Papa est en bas, qui coupe du bois ....

Go to sleep, Nick (Colas is short for Nicolas), my little brother
Go to sleep, you'll have some hot milk
Mummy is upstairs baking a cake
Daddy is downstairs, cutting some wood ....

À la claire fontaine, à la claire fontaine
M'y allant promener
J'ai trouvè l'eau si belle que je m'y suis baigné
Il y a longtemps que je t'aime
Jamais je ne t'oublierai.

At the clear spring, at the clear spring
Going on a stroll
I found the water so beautiful that I took a swim
I have been loving you for a long time
I will never forget you.

Au clair de la lune, mon ami Pierrot
Prêtes-moi ta plume, pour écrire un mot
Ma chandelle est morte, je n'ai plus de feu
Ouvres-moi ta porte, pour l'amour de Dieu.

In the moonlight, my friend, Pete
Lend me your pen to write a note
My candle went out, and I don't have a light
Open your door, for the love of God.

Une chanson douce que me chantait ma Maman
En suçant mon pouce tous les soirs en m'endormant
Cette chanson douce je la chanterai pour toi
Pour que ta nuit soit douce, tout là-bas au fond
des bois.

A tender song that my mummy sang for me
While I sucked my thumb every night falling asleep
This tender song I will sing for you
So that you'll have a good night, all the way in the
woods.

QUICK PAINLESS

Count your evening sheep in French. You'll wake up rested and another step closer to proficiency. *Un mouton, deux moutons, trois moutons ....*

Trucs of the Trade

Are you too lazy to read *Trucs* of the Trade?

1 The only time you use signs to communicate is when someone cuts you off on the road. ☐ yes ☐ no

2 You'd give all the *francs* in the world to pay a translator rather than learn a few words. ☐ yes ☐ no

3 Pointing and grunting has always gotten you what you need at home, why not in France, too? ☐ yes ☐ no

Chapter

three

Pointers for Success: Nonverbal Communication

Italians aren't the only people who use their hands to speak. A hand gesture can be worth a thousand words in any culture. In addition to hand gestures, subtle movements and even grunts can get your point across. If all else fails, there are some down-and-dirty last resorts I'll show you to make sure everyone will *comprendre* what you're saying (or signing, waving, pointing, and so on).

MARCEL MARCEAU SCHOOL FOR MIMES

If you are in a situation in which you're absolutely at a loss for words, don't try to use words. Sometimes a hand signal or another motion will work just as well. Here are a few gestures that mean the same thing in any language.

■ **Thumbs up.** A salesperson helps you find the sweater you are looking for, but you can't remember how to say so.

While watching a French movie or interacting with French people, pay close attention to gestures. When you were a child, you learned by imitating. Even now, you can learn gestures by imitating them. Just make sure you don't offend anyone!

What worked for Fonzie on *Happy Days* will work for you. Smile and give 'em a thumbs up.

- **Okay.** A waiter asks you how your meal is, and you blank out on the word for "good." Not a problem. Put your thumb and index finger together to indicate that things are okay.

- **Nod, smile, and say *oui*.** In a worst-case scenario, you'll probably do this instinctively to indicate assent. Nodding and smiling is always understood and always makes you seem like a most agreeable person.

- **Shake your head and say *non*.** Again, this probably will be your reflex when things are not as you'd like. Saying "no" with a head shake is understood almost everywhere in the world.

- **Stop sign.** If you don't want something, just put your hand up like a traffic cop and your intentions will be known.

- **Shrug.** Don't know what Pierre is talking about? Can't help someone who wants directions? Just raise your shoulders and the problem will go away.

- **Cock your head and lean forward to say you don't understand.** Have you ever spoken to a dog who was listening but not understanding you? This is the gesture he likely made. A look that says "Huh?" This is a good motion to use when you want something to be repeated for a second chance at understanding.

- **Bow to say thanks.** What works in Japan works in France, too. Bowing might be a somewhat formal way to communicate your gratitude, but you are always better off erring on the side of formality.

- **Toss your hand up and shrug to say it doesn't matter.** If you'll be happy seated here or there in the restaurant, indicate your indifference this way.

Last Resorts

Sometimes you have to get more detailed when you're in a bind and your simple gestures are not doing the trick. Here are a few of my favorite short cuts to being understood. They're not elegant and they're sometimes humbling, but they'll get the job done.

- **Charades.** If what you need can be acted out, you might have to wave your arms around to be understood, but at least the point will be made. For example, if you need a hair dryer, a *sèche-cheveux*, go to a housewares store and find an employee. Make the motion of holding a hair dryer to your head with one hand, shake your hair with your other hand, and make a whirring sound. It might not be a pretty sight, but it's easy to understand.

- **Write it down.** If you cannot communicate an address to a cab driver, write it down on a piece of paper and give it to him. If you are trying to make a phone call and can't figure out how to operate the phone, write down the number and gesture to a passerby that you need assistance.

A COMPLETE WASTE OF TIME

The 3 Worst Gestures You Can Make to a French Person:

1. Give him or her the finger. (This doesn't fly in any culture.)

2. Point at him with your index finger.

3. Brush your neck with your fingers to indicate indifference.

- **Hold a map and repeat a place name.** Don't be afraid to admit you're a tourist. This is the best way to get help when you are at a loss for words.

- **"Parlez-vous Anglais?"** ("Do you speak English?") Memorize this simple phrase and rely on the kindness of *étrangers*.

- **Resort to another language.** If your French has failed but you speak another language well, consider trying it. If you find someone who doesn't speak English, ask for assistance in Spanish, Italian, German, or any other language you might speak. Maybe you'll find someone else who speaks it, too.

- **Ask another tourist.** Let's say you are at the cathedral of Notre Dame and must find your way to the Louvre, but you do not think you can ask in French. Look around for another English-speaking tourist. At popular sites, you are likely to find someone who might not be a native but can help you just as well as one.

- **Me Tarzan, you Jane.** In a worst-case scenario, you can survive on nouns alone, miming the verbs or leaving them out entirely. If you stand around looking frantic and shouting *"Docteur!"* long enough, it will be understood that you need medical attention. When you don't even know the noun, you can say *"Comment dit-on?"* ("How does one say...?") and point or use English (or mongrel cognates). When you know more, you can use descriptive phrases such as "How do you say the thing you sleep on?" *"Comment dit-on la chose sur laquelle on dort?"*

YOU'LL THANK YOURSELF LATER

When traveling, always have a pen and paper handy. They can help you communicate, and you also can use them to write down new words or someone's address or phone number.

ACTIVITY: AU CINÉMA

I've always recommended to friends interested in learning French that they should watch all the French movies they can. *Le cinéma* is a French passion, so there are many good French movies out there. Happily, many of them are offered in the American market with subtitles.

I frequently hear complaints about how quickly the actors speak and how tough it is to truly understand. The goal is not to understand every word, however, but to pick up a few new words and to note how French sounds. Watching movies invariably helps your pronunciation, and it is ideal for picking up the gestures that the French use. Don't look for some esoteric sign language, you won't find it. What you will learn is how the French carry themselves. This will help you make yourself understood and welcomed in France.

In addition to picking up some of the language—both the spoken language and the body language—movies enable you to pick up some culture. You'll see how the French live, what they are interested in, and how they interact with one another. You also might discover new places you'd like to go or subjects you'd like to know more about. Here are just a few of my favorite movies:

IF YOU'RE SO INCLINED

If you are desperate to find someone who speaks English, go to the nearest hotel or American Express office. You are sure to find someone there.

Un Coeur en Hiver	*Jean de Florette*
Queen Margot	*Manon of the Spring*
Diva	*My Father's Glory*
A Man and a Woman	*My Mother's Castle*
The Last Metro	*Au Revoir les Enfants*

Tous les Matins du Monde	*The Double Life of Véronique*
Betty Blue	*And God Created Woman*
Mon Oncle	*L'Age d'Or*
Indochine	*La Chèvre*
La Belle Noiseuse	*La Discrète*
Camille Claudel	*La Grande Illusion*
Black Orpheus	*Ridicule*
Zazie dans le Metro	*French Twist*

Sometimes Hollywood directors and writers get lazy and decide to remake French films in English with American actors. If you are familiar with the American remakes listed here, you might want to rent the French originals. You'll already know the story from the remake, so you can focus on the language rather than the basic plot points. French movies remade in English include:

La Cage Aux Folles (The Birdcage)

La Femme Nikita (Point of No Return)

Three Men and a Cradle (Three Men and a Baby)

The Return of Martin Guerre (Sommersby)

La Totale (True Lies)

Cousin/Cousine (Cousins)

Les Diaboliques (Diabolique)

A Bout de Souffle (Breathless)

Mon Père, Ce Héro (My Father the Hero)

Chapter four

If You Can't Join 'Em, Beat 'Em: Circumventing the System

We'd all like to read a language book, master the vocabulary words and exercises, and then visit the country in which the language is spoken. We'd like to navigate an exotic country effortlessly, feeling like a native and feeling right at home. As we've already agreed, however, this is not realistic. You'll no doubt find a time when, despite all the hard work you've done learning some French, it's not enough. This chapter reveals some tricks and tips you can use to beat the system when you're in a jam. Many of this chapter's lessons are detailed in greater length in the body of the book. Consider these pages an introduction to *The Lazy Way* of getting the most benefit from the least amount of language acumen.

USE COGNATES

Chapter 6 of this book introduces you to cognates. Because French and English share a common background in Latin and ancient Greek, many words are similar or the same. These words are called cognates. Cognates can get you through many a jam.

As we'll discuss in Chapter 6, cognates are easy to find. If your French fails you, fall back on English and just use a French accent. After a few tries, you'll likely locate a cognate.

SINGLE PARTS OF SPEECH

Communicating with just one part of speech under your belt is not elegant, but it can be done. If you're in a pinch, you probably can get by just using words instead of sentences. If you must speak, you probably are looking for a person, place, or thing. Try using a combination of the noun you know you want and a gesture to indicate for what you need it. If you are in a pharmacy and need a Band-Aid, for example, if you know the word for arm, *bras*, you might point to the scrape on your arm and say, "*Mon bras*," indicating that you need a Band-Aid for it. If you are looking for the Louvre, you could say to someone "*Le Louvre?*" and then shrug your shoulders and look around, indicating that you are lost and need directions.

THE STREETS ARE YOUR CHEAT SHEET

If you are at a loss for words, look around you. There are French words everywhere: on signs, maps, labels, and

elsewhere. Let's say you're standing in the middle of Paris, and you realize you've forgotten the word for subway. Walk around for a moment or two. Before long, you'll stumble upon an entrance to the underground marked "*Métro*." Bingo! Now you know how to say it. Sometimes it's that easy.

Be Marcel Marceau

Animals are able to tell people what they need, and they don't speak French. In a worst-case scenario, you can act out your needs. It might not be pretty, but it'll be understood. See Chapter 3, "Pointers for Success: Nonverbal Communication," for detailed instructions on the art of pantomime.

Trial and Error

Tourists usually have lots of time. If you must find your own way and have no clue how to ask for help, just try to do it yourself. Get on the bus without checking to see if it really is going in the right direction. You might be able to figure it out on your own—or you might end up on the wrong side of the river. Either way, you'll get a quick tour of the city, and you might even stumble upon something of interest while you do it. What is said of Venice is true of many places. The best way to get to know it is to get lost in it.

When in Rome

Take instruction from people around you. They probably are successfully doing whatever you need to accomplish. Watch them and learn. If you've forgotten what to say

YOU'LL THANK YOURSELF LATER

I cannot stress this enough: Before you visit *any* city you've never been to before, buy a map of that city. Also make sure to obtain good maps of the public transportation system.

on the phone, for example, eavesdrop on a French person at a public telephone. You'll appear to just be waiting in line. Try to pick out words you know you'll need to say. Listening, watching, and copying are great ways to learn and to be reminded of forgotten words. As they say, keep your eyes and ears open.

This also is great advice for social situations. In Europe, it's never bad to be quiet. Listen attentively and your company will be appreciated.

The Buddy System

See if you can hook up with English speakers who know more French than you do. This is a good way to make new friends and to benefit from other people's knowledge. Hotels and touristy restaurants are places where you'll find others in your situation who probably want to see the same sites you do. It's easy to approach someone who looks just as foreign as you do.

Tour Guides and Hotel Staff

Go on organized tours to learn about specific subjects that interest you. Try a bike tour of the country or a guided museum group. You might meet some fellow tourists to bond with, as previously mentioned. You'll also enjoy the opportunity to ask your guide for advice. Save up your questions and ask them at the end of the tour. Tour guides are trained to be helpful. They won't mind indulging you as long as your questions are brief and your thoughts organized.

If you're staying in a hotel, the staff at the front desk also can be very helpful. They meet thousands of tourists just like you every year. If you have a question, you can be certain it's been asked before! Don't hesitate to ask for help when choosing restaurants or when deciding which tourist sites to visit. You can even ask how to get where you want to go.

Speak English

I know this is a book about learning French, so I've probably sunk to a new low in the history of language books. The reality, however, is that many people in France speak English. Ask for help if you really need it—even if it's just to ask what a French word means—and don't stress out about doing so. French speakers—even savvy ones like you—aren't built in a day.

Here are some places where you'll easily find people who speak English.

QUICK ☎ PAINLESS

Create a cheat sheet for yourself. If you are worried about not being able to converse, the day before you go somewhere jot down on a piece of paper a few key vocabulary words that you think might come in handy.

- **Hotels.** Nearly every hotel in France boasts several people on staff who speak English. They are there to serve so take advantage of them.

- **Tourist offices.** If you are in a popular part of town, there probably will be a tourist kiosk or an American Express office nearby where people speak your language.

- **Hospitals.** Hospitals are accustomed to crisis situations of every stripe, and there are usually people on staff who speak many languages.

- **Universities.** English is a very popular second language in France. There are bound to be English speakers in the neighborhood.

WHAT TO AVOID

The Lazy Way to learn a language, as you will see, is to pick and choose useful terms to learn and avoid those that will only hinder you. Beginners usually are taught the words for items that surround them. This usually means blackboards, windows, pens, and so on because they are in a classroom. When you use other books to teach yourself more French, keep this in mind. Look for books that teach you about real-life situations, not classroom ones. Unless you are a dog breeder, you probably don't need to know the word for dog. Unless you are a teacher on a mission to learn about French classrooms, don't bother learning the words for items found in schools. What you don't know is as important as what you do.

AT THE VERY LEAST

Here are the vocabulary words and phrases that I consider most useful:

I need ….	*J'ai besoin de ….*
I would like ….	*Je voudrais ….*
I'm lost.	*Je suis perdu.*
Is there ….	*Est-ce-qu'il y a ….*
Where is ….	*Ou est ….*
Do you speak English?	*Parlez-vous Anglais?*
Help me! (in case of emergencies)	*Aidez-moi!*

Congratulations! You've realized that there are clever ways to leverage your little bits of knowledge to great effect. Pop in a French movie and relax with a glass of wine.

The Lazy Way

ACTIVITY: HANGMAN

Remember how much fun you used to have playing hangman as a kid. The challenge probably wore off as you grew up. Well it's back. Since you don't know much French, hangman has once again, become a good way of strengthening your budding vocabulary. In this version, there are a few new rules.

1. You must select your letters in French. This way you will get used to saying the letters and your friend will get used to hearing them, and vice versa when you switch places.

2. The person drawing the hanging man and writing the letters must announce which body part he or she is drawing. For instance: *"Je dessine la tete."* ("I am drawing the head.")

3. You can draw as many body parts as it takes for your friend to guess the word. This will move you beyond arm and legs and may reinforce body parts as diverse as fingers, toes, and hair, depending on how well you play.

4. You may give hints if your friend is having trouble guessing the word, but all the hints must be in French. For instance, *"C'est un animal."* (It's an animal.) or *"C'est un verbe."* (It's a verb.)

QUICK **IN** *PAINLESS*

Learning French will be more enjoyable if you study with a friend.

Chapter five

A Method to the Madness: How to Make All You Know Stick

The most disheartening part of learning a new language is forgetting it. You'll be shocked at how easily words go in one ear and out the other. Sometimes it feels like you forget words almost before you learn them. Believe me, I know. This happened to me all the time when I was struggling to learn English. Do not lose heart! There are several *Lazy Ways to* make sure French remains at the forefront of your brain.

EXTRA! EXTRA! SUBSCRIBE TO A FRENCH NEWSPAPER

Plenty of French papers are available in America. One of the best for beginners is called *France-Amérique*. Its content is geared toward French speakers (and learners) living in America. Keeping up with a French newspaper helps you

know what the French are talking about and concerned with. Sometimes a French newspaper subscription can feel like a gym membership. You sign up for it, are enthusiastic about it for a month, and then watch it languish unused. Don't beat yourself up. Even if you just glance at the headlines or read an article now and then, this can be a useful tool in keeping your skills sharp.

The Buddy System: Join a French Group

Join your local Alliance Française or a local French film society. Even if you take advantage of it only a few times a year, you'll keep up on what's going on in your French community. Any time you use it, you'll be that much closer to mastering more French.

Play to Learn

Play games with yourself to keep you on your toes (*en pointe*—toe shoes in ballet). The games in this book are fun—notice the sidebars throughout and the sections at the end of each chapter. They include activities such as translating American song lyrics into French, counting sheep in French, and other wacky but cute tricks that work some French into your everyday life.

Trick or Treat: Fooling Your Memory

Think of clever, fun ways to remember the words you learn. Even if your methods don't make sense to others, if they help you keep some French in mind, you'll be ahead of the game. For instance, *gronder* means "to scold" in French. Children get grounded when they are in trouble. Although the words have nothing in common and are unrelated, forcing a connection between them enables you to remember an extra French word that might otherwise have eluded you.

Sortez Une Feuille de Papier: Take Out a Piece of Paper

When French high school teachers say this, it elicits a groan from the students. Taking out a piece of paper means taking a quiz. In your case, it means testing yourself. That's right. If you have a disciplined streak, you might want to buy a French workbook and force your way through it. Some people prefer the structure and breadth that a workbook provides. If you are such a person, create a schedule for yourself and take some time every week to do one set of exercises. Enough repetition will force some words and bits of grammar to stick.

Get a Move On: Book a Trip

Research your next trip to France—even if it's a long way off. As you plan, speak to yourself in French about the fabulous places you'll go, the people you'll meet, and the adventures you'll have.

Surround Sound: Listen to Music

Listening to French music (and language tapes, if that's your pleasure) in your spare time is a great way to get enthusiastic and to brush up on your skills. You can listen while you are doing other things: driving to work, exercising, cooking dinner, or cleaning the house, for example. If your treadmill is in front of a TV, you can rent French movies to strengthen your calves and your French

IF YOU'RE SO
INCLINED

Keep your guidebooks handy even if you don't have a trip planned. Thumbing through them and daydreaming is one of the best ways to make sure you'll see French words in your off-season. My favorite guidebook is Patricia Wells's *Food Lover's Guide to Paris*.

at the same time. It is absolutely the most fun way I can think of to bolster your vocabulary and to keep words in your head. Think about the way children learn—music is an important part of grade school.

These are some of the French-language singers that the French students I know like best.

Classic Crooning

Yves Montand

This actor/singer got his start on the stage in Marseilles. He became a darling of Paris and eventually of Hollywood. Check out his movies as well as his songs, the latter of which are romantic and old-fashioned.

Maurice Chevalier

Another actor/singer from an older generation, Chevalier is famous for his role in *Gigi*. Like Rex Harrison or Yul Brynner, he half-sings, half-speaks his songs. This makes him easy to understand, but the music is a bit more dated than Montand's.

Edith Piaf

This songbird of Paris is the emblem of French *chansons*. Her music, although as old as Chevalier's, sounds timeless. It's so atmospheric that beginners love to listen and imagine, sing along to "*La Vie en Rose*," and try to imagine that they're at a sidewalk cafe in Paris.

Charles Aznavour

Alive and kicking, Aznavour is arguably the last of the great crooners. He's the French Sinatra. *"Jazznavour"* is my favorite album of his.

Charles Trenet

Trenet is another classic French singer whose music I love.

Jacques Brel

Ditto for Jacques. His music is a bit dated, but it's still an ideal pick for practicing the difficult "r" pronunciation.

Mireille Mathieu

If you like Edith Piaf, you'll like Mathieu.

Cheesy European Music

Christophe

It doesn't get any cheesier than this. If you like Barry Manilow, Christophe's your guy.

Patricia Kaas

She's got a slight 1970s lounge edge to her, but she sings clearly and with feeling.

Pascal Obispo

Same story. A little campy but fine.

Celine Dion

Before she learned English and made zillions of dollars, Celine sang in French. If she's your cup of tea, sip some of her French work.

IF YOU'RE SO
INCLINED

Don't expect to understand a song the first time you hear it. Just sing first, understand later!

Listen to French music with a dictionary, pen, and paper by your side. Use the listening experience as a dictation exercise. Try to write down what the singer says and see if you can make sense of it.

Lara Fabian

If you like Celine, you'll like Lara.

Hipster Style

Serge Gainsbourg

A huge star, Gainsbourg was the coolest thing around in the 1960s and 1970s. I love his velvet voice and loungey arrangements. I don't know anyone who knows his music and doesn't like it.

Jane Birkin

Birkin is British, but she married Gainsbourg and launched a career singing in French. I think she's just as cool as Gainsbourg.

Françoise Hardy

Another great singer and cool personality. I often listen to my many Françoise Hardy CDs.

Random Pop

Jean Louis Murat

Cool and laidback, Murat is easy to understand, and his music is lyrical and contemporary. My favorite album, "Cheyenne Autumn" (odd that the title is in English), comes with liner notes.

Alain Bashung

This is very mellow rock. I recommend the album "*Fantaisie Militaire*," which is good and has liner notes with lyrics.

Jazz

Paris Combo

A great jazz band. If you are hosting a jazz brunch, put this in to brush up on your French as you eat your *croissants*.

Claude Nougaro

I'd call this peppy jazz. The music is upbeat, and the words are comprehensible.

Michel Jonasz

This is jazzy stuff with very clear lyrics. Jonasz has a lovely voice that's ideal for a beginner trying to understand French.

Jacques Higelin

This is a very funky singer. It's like jazz with a hard edge. Higelin reminds me of a teenager going through a difficult phase. Despite this, his elocution is excellent—he does a lot of talk-singing—and is perfect for working on your accent.

Offbeat

Fatal Mambo

French lyrics with a Latin beat. This group is lively and fun yet still easy to understand.

MC Solaar

French rap. You might think the words in a rap song would be easier to understand than those of another kind of song. Not true. This is tough to understand

QUICK ◼ PAINLESS

If your CDs come with liner notes, you can follow along with the singer. Bilingual CD notes (lyrics in both French and English) help a great deal.

and full of slang, but if rap's your thing, it is available *en français*.

Cafe de Paris

Accordion music. Wait! Keep reading. This music actually is really cute and very atmospheric. Some of it is instrumental; some is vocal. It's all a hoot.

ACTIVITY: DO ONE OF THE ABOVE

You don't have to wait until you're finished with this book to start finding ways to practice your French. Pick the activity that most appeals to you from this chapter and see how far you can take it.

IF YOU'RE SO
INCLINED

If you want your home to feel like one of those Audrey Hepburn movies set in Paris, get some accordion music.

Français, Clair and Simple (French, Clear and Simple): Projects

Are you too lazy to read *Français, Clair and Simple (French, Clear and Simple): Projects*?

1 You thought only people were masculine and feminine, not things like books and chairs. ☐ yes ☐ no

2 The only verb you have any interest in is regardez (to watch) as in regardez la télévision. ☐ yes ☐ no

3 The closest you'll get to French fashion (la mode) is eating your brownies with ice cream on top (à la mode). ☐ yes ☐ no

Chapter

six

You Already Speak French: Cognates

Good news, you already speak French! *Comment?* (What?) It's true. A number of words are exactly the same in French as they are in English, and others are very similar. These are called cognates. You might not have recognized these friends in the past because they are pronounced differently, but now that you've learned the French alphabet, you'll have a much easier time recognizing and using them.

FRIENDS: THE FRENCH YOU ALREADY KNOW

In addition to cognates, some French words have infiltrated everyday English. Ever eaten a tasty *hors d'oeuvre* at a swanky *soirée?* Ever had a *tête-à-tête* with a friend? See, you already know lots of French. This chapter will show you how to capitalize on all this knowledge.

Let's follow some time-worn advice: Know your friends and know your enemies. First, we'll get reacquainted with some old friends. We'll show you some cognates you'll recognize in

In the privacy of your own home, try speaking with a French accent. Look at the things around you and say them the way a French person would. You might stumble upon a few cognates as you perfect your accent.

their English clothes. We'll then drape them in French garb and admire the expanded possibilities of your wardrobe. We'll even show you how to mix and match your words and endings to create French words you never knew you knew! We call this process, very unscientifically, Frenchification. We'll also meet some *faux amis*, or false friends. These are words that appear to translate back and forth but that actually have very different meanings.

Bingo: Exact Cognates

These words are old friends. They translate exactly between English and French. To use them, you need only to practice your new pronunciation skills and budding French accent. When you are trying to think of the French word for something, always check for an exact cognate first. Simply take the English word and say it with a French accent.

English	French	Phonetic
accident	*accident*	ack-sea-dahn
bandage	*bandage*	bahn-dahje
bus	*bus*	boos
cigarette	*cigarette*	sea-gahr-ette
cinema	*cinéma*	sea-nay-mah
idiot	*idiot*	ee-dee-oh
taxi	*taxi*	tahk-si
telephone	*téléphone*	tay-lay-fun
important	*important*	am-pour-tahn
simple	*simple*	sehm-pleh

CLOSE: SIMILAR COGNATES

Okay, so maybe there's not an exact cognate, and the Parisian gentleman you were speaking to furrowed his brow in misunderstanding. No matter. Here we'll introduce you to some new friends. These cognates are not exact, but they come close enough to prove very helpful to a French student like you. As you read through the list of close cognates, try to focus on the patterns. Certain English endings tend to translate into particular French endings. We'll discuss the transition patterns in more detail later in this chapter. Right now, you should focus on the concept of making slight adjustments to Frenchify and find a close cognate.

English	French	Phonetic
bank	*banque*	bahnk
city	*cité*	sea-tay
museum	*musée*	moo-zay
park	*parc*	pahrke
absolutely	*absolument*	ab-so-loo-mawn
clear	*clair*	claire
necessary	*nécessaire*	neh-seh-saire
serious	*sérieux*	sea-ree-oo
explain	*expliquer*	ex-plee-kay

There might be a cognate for what you're trying to say, but it might not be the one on the tip of your tongue. Rack your brains for synonyms. One of them might work. For example, if you try to Frenchify the word "mistake" by pronouncing it with a French accent, you won't be understood. When you try again with *erreur*, however, you will.

For example, if you want to say "car" to a Parisian. You Frenchify it into *carré* or *carte*. Still nothing, just a blank stare. You might be lazy, but you're determined. You put on your best French accent and try *auto* or *véhicule*. *Exactement!* You are rewarded with understanding in either case.

NO CIGAR: FALSE FRIENDS

By now, we hope you're fairly well convinced that French really is easy. Hold tight to that belief because confidence is half the battle. As in any battle, however, enemies lurk in the midst. Beware of the false friend or, as they are called in French, *faux amis*. These words appear to be cognates but they're not. Their meanings do not travel to and from France so neatly in your *valise*. Do not despair, but do realize that a few of these words exist. If you choose one by mistake, you'll probably elicit a laugh and a confused look. You then can attempt to choose a synonym that conveys your meaning more successfully.

French	False	True
bourdon	burden	bumblebee
chair	chair	flesh
librairie	library	book shop
magasin	magazine	store
pain	pain	bread

toile	toil	cloth, canvas
attirer	to dress	to attract, to lure
balader	to sing	to stroll, to walk
fondre	to like	to melt, to dissolve
travailler	to travel	to work

FRENCHIFICATION: MAKING YOUR OWN CLOSE COGNATES

You've seen the Frenchification process at work in the preceding tables. Try these neat tricks to Frenchify words with endings that lend themselves to translation. Note

English	Ending	French	Phonetic
-or	-eur	*docteur*	dock-tewer
-er	-re	*théâtre*	tay-ah-tre
-ist	-iste	*artiste*	ar-teest
-ed	-e	*fatigué*	fah-tee-gay
-est	-este, -et	*déteste*	day-test
-id	-ide	*humide*	ooh-mee-de
-em	-ème	*problème*	praw-bleh-me
-and	-ande	*demande*	deh-mawn-de
-ial	-iel	*officiel*	ohfee-see-ahl
-ic	-ique	*publique*	poo-bleek

QUICK ◼ *PAINLESS*

Go formal. In making cognates, think of the most proper word you can. When you think of the word "trip," for example, it is a very casual and not-so-specific meaning for what you want to say. What is a grander, more formal equivalent? *Voyage*.

that these are rules of thumb and not rules, per se. Using these patterns to determine the meanings of words you hear and to create words yourself is very helpful, but they are patterns, and patterns can have irregularities.

Read the words in the table on the preceding page aloud in English and in French. Try to recognize the way the sounds change from one language to the other. Some people like to picture the spelling transition; others simply hear the migration. Use whatever works best for you.

Pretty neat, eh? Remember, the idea is not to memorize the endings or to view them as gospel but to recognize the sounds and letter combinations that make French words unique.

In addition to word endings, there are other tip-offs to understanding French. Vowels sometimes appear in French words with an accent over them: ô, ê, and so on. This can signify an English equivalent from which an "s" has been removed. For example, the French word *forêt* corresponds to the English word forest. The French word *bête* corresponds to the English beast. The next time you see an ê combination, try inserting an "s" after the ê to see whether the English meaning becomes apparent.

FINDING YOUR ROOTS: EXTRACTING MEANING

Whether you believe in the Big Bang or the Garden of Eden, we all had to start somewhere and so did language. English and French both use certain roots inherited from Latin and Greek ancestors. Not only does this shared origin help in producing exact and close cognates as previously discussed, it also helps us find meaning in certain less familiar looking and sounding words.

Identifying the common roots of words is a helpful way to ease yourself into French. Roots are very useful as you learn and when you have the time to figure things out, such as when you are reading a sign.

Let's take the very word we've been discussing—cognate—to show you how roots work. Cognates are words of a similar nature or of the same family. Are there other, more familiar English words you can think of that share its root and approach its meaning? How about the word "recognize"? To recognize means to see something and remember where it came from or where you saw it before. Now look at the French verb *connaître*. It means to know or to be acquainted with. Knowing that the word "recognize" has to do with identification can help you figure out and remember the gist of *connaître*.

Consider these other words with roots common to both French and English:

- *Dormir.* Did your college have dorms? What were they for? Sleeping. Bingo! Dormir means to sleep.

- *Bibliothèque.* Anything familiar here? How about bibliography? A bibliography is where you list books you've consulted for your research paper. Hence *biblo-* relates to books. What else relates to books? Libraries; it's a library. (If you thought of a bookstore first, give yourself a pat on the back; you are starting to see how roots work.)

A COMPLETE WASTE OF TIME

Unless you are a very abstract thinker, thinking about the roots of words is not helpful in conversation because things move very quickly.

■ *Vivre.* Do you know any vivacious—or lively—people? Ever found a party's atmosphere to be convivial—or lively? That's right, *vivre* means to live.

The Import/Export Business: Words That Have Traveled

Roots are not the only thing we've borrowed. The English language has absorbed many French words and phrases just as they are—with their French spellings and their French pronunciations intact. The exchange works the other way, too. To many a proper Frenchman's chagrin, English creeps further and further into the French language and culture. In our concerted yet lazy effort to learn French, it pays to exploit the import/export trade, getting all the French we can from what we already know and say.

Some Parisians in America:

apéritif	concierge	liaison
attaché	connaisseur	malaise
banquet	cuisine	née
bouquet	couchette	premier
bustier	coup	soirée
café	encore	valise
charade	ennui	vogue
chic	ensemble	voyeur

Phrases and Expressions:

déjà vu—the familiar feeling of having "already seen" something

maître d'hôtel—master of the hotel

raison d'être—reason to exist

pince nez—eyeglasses that "pinch the nose"

laissez-faire—the perfect lazy mantra; literally, " leave to do"

ç'est la vie—that's life

faux pas—a gaff: literally, a "false step"

tête-à-tête—a conversation; literally, a "head to head"

entre nous—between us

à la mode—in the fashion (fashionable)

carte blanche—complete discretion; literally, "white card"

eau de toilette—grooming water (perfume)

je ne sais quoi—I don't know what

joie de vivre—joy of living

au revoir—until we see one another again

film noir—a movie with a dark streak; literally, a "black film"

bon voyage—have a good trip

café au lait—coffee with milk

chaise longue—long chair

savoir-faire—savvy. Literally, "to know to do."

IF YOU'RE SO
INCLINED

"Laissez-faire" is also an economics term in English. It denotes a conscious policy of allowing the marketplace to set its own rules.

s'il vous plait—please. Literally, "If it pleases you"

haute couture—high fashion

AMERICANS ABROAD: ENGLISH WORDS IN FRENCH

The French, you might have heard, are protective of the beauty of their language. The *Académie Française* has gone to excruciating pains to keep the French language as pure as possible. Despite its efforts, a number of English words are still understood and frequently used in France. You'll note that many of the American imports are in the fields of technology and pop culture—fields in which Americans are on the cutting edge.

Americans in Paris:

weekend

rock and roll

show biz

Internet

blockbuster

fax

supermodel

CULTURE CLUB: LET YOUR GUIDEBOOK TEACH YOU FRENCH

A fun way to bolster your French vocabulary is to figure out what French place names, books, works of art, and even brands mean. As you plan your next trip to France or as you enjoy French culture from your American armchair, see whether you can add to your vocabulary by dissecting famous names.

Famous Places

Île de la Cité	Isle of the City
Comédie-Française	French Comedy
Pont Neuf	New Bridge
Arc de Triomphe	Arch of Triumph
La Tour Eiffel	Eiffel's Tower
Place des Invalides	Square of the Invalids
Palais Royal	Royal Palace
Rive Gauche	Left Bank
Notre Dame	Our Lady

Art and Literature

La Bohème (Puccini opera)	The Bohemian
Le Penseur (Rodin sculpture)	The Thinker
Les Misérables (Victor Hugo book)	The Miserable (Ones)

Brand

Bain de Soleil	Sun Bath

IN PRACTICE: EXERCISES

Q: How do you get to *l'Opéra Bastille?*

A: Practice, practice, practice.

It's true—practice makes perfect. But fear not. In addition to being *The Lazy Way* to learn French, this is the fun way. Try these very simple exercises at your leisure to reinforce your ability to use cognates.

- Look around your house, your yard, or wherever you like and try to Frenchify or find cognates for the things you see. Look in your French/English *dictionnaire* to see how close you came.

- Think of other French expressions or place names in addition to the ones mentioned in the preceding sections. Try to figure out their literal meanings by breaking them into parts. Use a French guidebook if you are having trouble brainstorming.

ACTIVITY: MAD LIBS

To practice your Frenchification skills, fill in the blanks in the following story with cognates. Don't worry if you don't come up with the exact words the author might have had in mind. As long as you use cognates that make some sort of sense, you'll be getting some practice and some laughs!

Once upon a time, a lady named Jeanne lived in an <u>noun</u> in Paris, France all alone except for her <u>number</u> <u>plural noun</u>. Jeanne was a very fat and lonely woman. She was retired and did not get out much. For her, going to the <u>noun</u> was an event of <u>adjective</u> proportions. She often cursed at the cashiers there just to make <u>noun</u>.

One day, as Jeanne was walking along the Seine on her way home from the store, she slipped and fell into the <u>noun</u>. As the dirty water engulfed her, she cried out for <u>noun</u>.

Henri was bicycling along the river when he heard her <u>plural noun</u> for help. He stopped, leaned his <u>noun</u> against a <u>noun</u>, and rushed down to <u>verb</u> her. Pulling Jeanne to shore was a <u>adjective</u> task for <u>adjective</u> Henri due to her <u>adjective</u> size. After much effort, he succeeded.

When the two <u>past tense verb</u> to the banks of the Seine, covered in muddy water, they discovered that Henri's bike had been stolen. *"Zut, alors!"* he cried. Jeanne was so grateful to him for saving her that she <u>past tense verb</u> to buy him a <u>adjective</u> bike. This <u>adjective</u> deed inspired Jeanne to become a happier, more balanced woman. She resolved never to bark at the cashiers again.

seven

You Say Potato, I Say *Pomme de Terre:* Nouns

Now that you've been reacquainted with many old friends, it's time to learn some new ones. Nouns are, *bien sûr* (of course), one of the most basic parts of speech. Once you've mastered them, you'll be on your way to speaking French.

This chapter introduces you to nouns you'll use in everyday speech. This chapter contains a lot of vocabulary, but don't worry, we'll show you how to have fun as you commit it to memory. We won't cover all common nouns in this chapter (or even in the whole book), so remember to use your Frenchification skills and diligence to add your own nouns. You'll also meet other nouns throughout the book as we cover related topics such as dining, travel, and so on.

LADIES AND GENTLEMEN: NOUNS HAVE GENDER

Unlike their English counterparts, French nouns have gender. The French refer to an object as he or she, depending on its

gender. The same is true for plural nouns. Even "the" is indicative of gender in France. "I'm confused," you say. "How can a table be female?" The answer is that it just is. Don't try to find a pattern for which objects are which gender. There isn't one.

Don't drive yourself crazy trying to remember the gender of everything—just try one or the other or both. For homemade cognates, you just have to guess. You'll get the gender wrong much of the time, but so what? You'll still be able to get your point across, and objects don't get offended when you mistake them for the opposite sex. But people do!

Articles

These are the definite articles I recommend you learn. The word "the" is as useful in France as it is in the United States.

the:

le (m)

la (f)

les (m/f plural)

You'll notice that articles change depending on the gender of the nouns they accompany, but there's only one plural for "the."

Yours, Mine, and Ours: Possession

You're learning French the easy way. The easiest and best way to say who something belongs to is to use the preposition *à* with personal pronouns. The construction *c'est à* + pronoun enables you to indicate ownership in an easy and perfectly acceptable way.

Personal Pronouns

moi

toi

lui

nous

vous

leur/elles

Examples:

Whose book is it?   *Le livre, c'est à moi.*
The book is mine.

Whose guitar is it? *La guitare, c'est à elles.*
The guitar is theirs (f).

OUT WITH A BANG: ENDINGS

As in English, the plural form of a French noun usually is just the singular form with an "s" on the end. In certain cases, however, you need more than the final "s." If the word ends in a vowel other than "e," you'll need to finesse a bit more. Words ending in "u" require an additional "x."

Examples:

la guerre, les guerres   the wars

le chapeau, les chapeaux   the hats

A COMPLETE WASTE OF TIME

The 3 Worst Things You Can Do with Noun Genders:

1. Spend hours trying to detect a pattern for which nouns are which gender.

2. Not laugh heartily enough at your mistakes and learn from them.

3. Not worry about gender at all, thus extending your errors to nouns for people.

If you are interested in eventually mastering written French, pay attention to the spellings of plural endings. You can even exaggerate the subtle phonetic differences in pronunciation while learning, to help you visualize the different spellings in your mind.

Don't worry about adding the correct plural suffix to French words. When speaking, no one can tell a final "x" from an "s" in the same spot. These subtle adjustments are for written French. As lazy learners, we need only to communicate—and *The Lazy Way* works.

AEIOU: VOWELS

The French are lazy just like you. They enjoy speaking quickly and efficiently and adjust their language accordingly. They do this by vowel blending, elision, and vowel endings.

Vowel Blending

When two vowels meet at an intersection of two words, the French combine them into one sound. Both *le* and *la* become *l'*. "H" is silent in the vowel blend.

Examples:

J'habite	Je + habite
L'accident	Le + accident
C'est	Ce + est

Don't drive yourself crazy trying to spell every vowel blend that arises. Instead, focus on the way French sounds. Let the vowels run into each other as they roll off your tongue. Don't worry about spelling.

Elision

Elision occurs when an "s" falls at the end of a word that is followed by another word beginning with a vowel. Although the final French "s" generally is silent, when it is succeeded by a vowel, it is pronounced and serves as an effective bridge to the next word. The same is true for the French "x."

Examples:

les idées absurdes	lee-zi-day-zahb-serde
faux amis	foe-zah-mees
les beaux-arts	lay-bowse-zar

Enunciation

Final consonants such as "t," "n," and "l," usually are not pronounced in France. As in elision, these sounds only are said when coupled with vowels. This is frequently the case as a result of gender changes.

Examples:

brun, brune	brehn, broon
fort, forte	for, fort
naturel, naturelle	nah-teu-rel, nah-teur-elle

LA MÉNAGERIE

Although you might never visit a French family farm, you'll still find conversational use for the nouns for animals whether you're discussing food or the family pet (which I hope is not one and the same). Here are a few frequently used words for our fine feathered and furry friends.

pet	*l'animal* (m)
bird	*l'oiseau* (m)

IF YOU'RE SO INCLINED

Practice your vowel blending, elision, and enunciation skills and have some fun by assembling your own French tongue-twisters. Mix and match some of the words and phrases you know into amusing examples of these pronunciation skills.

cat	*le chat*
cow	*la vache*
chicken	*le poulet*
dog	*le chien*
duck	*le canard*
fish	*le poisson*
goose	*l'oie (f)*
horse	*le cheval*
mouse	*la souris*

IT'S ALL IN WHO YOU KNOW

No man is an island, as they say. We all relate to one another in some way. As such, you'll need to refer to the people in your life as well as to people you meet on the street. First you'll learn the basic words for people, and then you'll discover how to relate them to yourself.

Les Autres (The Others)

man	*l'homme*
woman	*la femme*
child	*l'enfant* (m/f)
baby	*le bébé*
adult	*l'adulte* (m/f)

La Famille (The Family)

mother	*la mère*
father	*le père*

wife	*la femme*
husband	*le mari*
spouse	*l'époux, l'épouse*
son	*le fils*
daughter	*la fille*
brother	*le frère*
sister	*la sœur*
uncle	*l'oncle*
aunt	*la tante*
grandfather	*le grand-père*
grandmother	*la grand-mère*
in-law	add *beau/belle*, as in *belle-fille* (daughter-in-law) and *beau-fils* (son-in-law)
friend	*l'ami* (m), *l'amie* (f)
significant other	*le petit ami*

Exercise:

Build your family tree. Draw it out on paper and fill in the branches with the names of your relatives. Read the tree by saying "*Mon* (m) or *ma* (f) [fill in noun] *c'est* [fill in name]." For example, "*Mon frère, c'est Nicolas.*" Go through the list several times, picturing each person as you say the French word for their relation to you. Repeat the exercise until you become comfortable with the new terms.

AROUND THE HOUSE

Whether you are staying in a hotel or are lucky enough to enjoy the home of a French *ami*, you'll need to get around the facility. These basic terms for the rooms should help.

kitchen	*la cuisine*
bathroom	*la salle de bains*
toilet	*les toilettes* (always plural)
living room	*le salon*
dining room	*la salle à manger*
bedroom	*la chambre*
attic	*le grenier*
basement	*le sous-sol*
staircase	*l'escalier* (m)
upstairs	*en haut*
downstairs	*en bas*
house	*la maison*
apartment	*l'appartement* (m)
garage	*le garage*

Here's another word to the washroom wise: fast-food facilities usually are conveniently located and are easy to identify. You'll likely recognize the layout of the place and find familiar accommodations. Have it your way!

STOLEN PARTS

As you proceed to the next two chapters and meet other parts of speech, you'll still want to have nouns on the

QUICK ⬭ PAINLESS

Do you need to use the restroom? You might not recognize the abbreviation on the restroom door in France. Having read this book, however, even the lazy will be prepared to find relief. As in England, the letters "WC" often mark the door of *les toi-lettes*. This stands for "water closet," a word that has emigrated from England to France.

brain. As in most languages, in French, it usually is a relatively simple task to convert between parts of speech. Even though we did not specifically learn the noun for something, you might be able to figure it out by knowing the related verb or adjective.

Examples:

verb—*travailler*	noun—*le travail*
(to work)	(work)
adjective—*dangereux*	noun—*le danger*
(dangerous)	(danger)

Be creative. Don't be afraid to make mistakes—trial and error can work for you. The more familiar you become with the language and the way it sounds, the fewer attempts you'll need to effectively convey your meaning.

ACTIVITY: SYNONYMS AND ANTONYMS

A fun way to remember vocabulary words is to think of them in terms of synonyms (words that have the same meaning as each other) and antonyms (words that are the opposite of each other). Fill in the following table.

Word	Synonym	Antonym
ancien	_____	*jeune*
seul	_____	*marié*
grand	*haut*	_____
agréable	_____	*méchant*
jolie	*belle*	_____

IF YOU'RE SO

INCLINED

Haul out your French dictionary and look up one item for each room in the house. For example, look up the word "razor" for the bathroom item. Can you guess how to say "razor" in French? This is a great way to confirm cognates as well as to pick up a few new terms.

The Good, the Bad, and the Ugly: Adjectives

You don't really need adjectives in your life, but a life without them is drab and without color, quantity, and size. Would you rather receive a rose or a big bunch of long-stemmed, red roses? In the land of *amour* and *joie de vivre*, you'll be happy to have adjectives under your belt.

Adjectives do more than just add color to your life. You can use adjectives to modify nouns. With a few choice adjectives in your employ, you can watch your *vocabulaire* grow from *petit* to *grand*.

COLOR ME FRENCH: COLORS

Many great works of art have come from French palettes including those of Claude Monet and Henri Matisse. Consider these beauties.

rouge	red
orange	orange

jaune	yellow
vert	green
bleu	blue
violet	purple
rose	pink
brun	brown
noir	black
blanc	white

Exercise:

Here's a fun way to practice your number and color skills. Create your own paint-by-number picture. Organize a crayon set of the preceding 10 colors and assign a French number to each. Use a children's coloring book unless you are particularly artistically inclined. Go through the coloring spaces and number them according to the colors you want them to be, using the list you just created. Write the appropriate numerals in each block. As you fill in the spaces, try to say the numbers and announce what color you are using in French. You should end up with a cute picture for your refrigerator and a working knowledge of the numbers 1–10 and basic colors.

ADJECTIVE PLACEMENT

In English, adjectives almost always precede the nouns to which they refer: the great chase, the naked city, and the first lady. In French, adjectives can either precede or follow the noun to which they refer. Although the majority of French adjectives usually follow their nouns, certain others usually precede them: *beau* (handsome) and *grand* (big), for example. For your purposes, we recommend that you keep things simple and put all adjectives after their nouns. This way, most will end up correctly placed. You'll get used to hearing the reversed order and eventually will be able to move the special adjectives you meet in front of the nouns as you learn them.

Examples:

le film sérieux
the serious film

les odeurs fortes
the strong odors

les hommes impulsifs
the impulsive men

la dame sans humour
the serious lady

la vie avec plaisir
the pleasurable life

les hommes sans idées
the men without ideas

BATTLE OF THE SEXES: GENDER ACCORD

In Chapter 7, you learned that French nouns are either masculine or feminine. It follows, then, that the adjectives modifying these nouns must agree. The rule of thumb is a simple one. If the noun is masculine, the modifying adjective also must be masculine. This is the practice of gender accord—agreement between

IF YOU'RE SO INCLINED

You can avoid adjectives by using nouns to describe nouns—just use the French words for with (*avec*) and without (*sans*). This also enables you to describe something even if you only know the word for the opposite of what you want to say.

Adjectives also need to agree with their nouns in terms of number. A singular noun requires a singular adjective; a plural noun requires a plural adjective.

the parts of speech in terms of gender. Use the same techniques you learned in Chapter 7 to make adjectives feminine or plural.

Examples:

le chapeau noir
the black hat

la chemise bleue
the blue shirt

les sandales rouges
the red sandals

BRIC-À-BRAC: VOCABULARY

The next series of *vocabulaire* introduces you to more adjectives you can use in everyday French speech (or practice). Try to use them as often as you can, tossing them right into your English for practice and modifying the French nouns you know.

People in Your Neighborhood

Masculine	Feminine	English
grand	grande	big
petit	petite	small
heureux	heureuse	happy
triste	triste	sad
haut	haute	tall
petit	petite	short

gentil	gentille	nice
méchant	méchante	mean
beau	belle	beautiful
laid	laide	ugly
mince	mince	thin
gros	grosse	fat
vieux	vieille	old
jeune	jeune	young
marié	mariée	married
célibataire	célibataire	single
blond	blonde	blond
châtain	châtain	brunette
riche	riche	rich
pauvre	pauvre	poor

Exercise:

Practice your adjectives while you do your errands. Notice the cashier at *le supermarché* and the other people in line at *la pharmacie*. Try to pick out one distinctive trait about each person. Use the trait to describe the people in your head. If you see a man with sad eyes, say to yourself, "There is *un homme triste*." Try to remember three people and how you described them. When you

YOU'LL THANK YOURSELF LATER

No language is crystal clear. Almost anything can stand further description. Spice up your conversation with adjectives!

get home, say the descriptive phrases aloud while pictur-ing the people that inspired them. You'll get better at adjectives and probably have a few laughs.

The Way Things Are

masculine	feminine	definition
ouvert	ouverte	open
fermé	fermée	closed
neuf	neuve	new
ancien	ancienne	old
bon	bonne	good
mauvais	mauvaise	bad
vrai	vraie	true
faux	fausse	false
court	courte	short
long	longue	long

THIS AND THAT: DEMONSTRATIVE ADJECTIVES

Which one do you want? Which blue one? To answer this type of inquiry, you'll need to put some demonstrative adjectives into your *poche* (pocket). These special adjectives go before the nouns they modify and, as always, must agree with the nouns in both gender and quantity.

Congratulations! You've just added the power of adjectives to your French skills. Relax and take a breather. Step outside and grab a breath of fresh air. You must take the time to smell the roses if you want to put your adjectives to work describing them!

The Lazy Way

ce (masculine)	this, that
cet (masculine)	this, that (before a vowel only)
cette (feminine)	this, that
ces (plural, m/f)	those

Examples:

J'aime ce chapeau.
I like this hat.

Elle voudrait acheter ces chemises.
She would like to buy those shirts.

Nous visitons cet architecte.
We are visiting that architect.

FOR BETTER OR WORSE: COMPARISONS

As in any language, you'll need to make comparisons in French. Luckily, doing so is relatively painless. The French use *plus ... que* and *moins ... que* to compare items. This is similar to how we use "more ... than" and "less ... than" in English. The superlative is just *le plus* (the most) or *le moins* (the least). To add emphasis in French, use the word *très*, which means very. These terms can be used with both adjectives and adverbs in French comparisons.

Examples:

Il est plus beau que Paul.
He is more handsome than Paul.

Elles sont moins grosses que nous.
They are less overweight than we.

QUICK PAINLESS

If you're a mnemonic fan, try using the acronym BAGS (beauty, age, goodness, size) to help you remember which adjectives precede their nouns. Remember, these are the exceptions—most adjectives follow their nouns.

Ce livre est très cher.
This book is very expensive.

C'est le plus cher.
That is the most expensive.

TRULY, MADLY, DEEPLY: ADVERBS

Just as you can use adjectives to modify nouns, you can describe verbs using adverbs. In most cases, once you know an adjective, you can convert it to an adverb by simply adding *-ment* to the ending. Like adjectives, adverbs follow the words they describe (with a few special exceptions). Let's try converting and using a few of these useful tools.

Adjective	Adverb	English
rapid	rapidement	quickly
lent	*lentement*	slowly
vrai	*vraiment*	truly, really
facile	*facilement*	easily
seul	*seulement*	only
complete	*complètement*	completely

Oddly: Irregular Adverbs

A number of adverbs exist *seulement* in adverbial form. Although we don't recommend that you devote hours to learning these exceptions, you should become familiar with some of the more popular irregular adverbs.

alors	then
aussi	too

comme	as
encore	again
enfin	finally
ensemble	together
ici	here
là	there
maintenant	now
souvent	often
toujours	always
tout	entirely
trop	too much

Examples:

Il pleut trop.
It rains too much.

Je vais souvent à l'opéra.
I often go to the opera.

Nous visitons ensemble.
We visit together.

ACTIVITY: CAT IN THE HAT GAME

Gather your favorite fellow French students for a guessing game. You'll only need a hat (or a bowl or something similar), paper and pens, and your finest French nouns to play. Divide into teams and have each player write down the names of famous French people, each on the same size slip of paper. Place the names in the hat and shake them.

QUICK ⬤ PAINLESS

Adverbs describe verbs. That's why the word "verb" is in their name. Why are words that describe nouns called adjectives? I don't know.

If your friends are learning French too, why not have a party with games like this one?

When it's your turn, draw a name from the hat and have your team members guess what name you hold by describing the celebrity with French nouns. Use a watch to impose a time limit that the group deems appropriate. Rotate turns until the hat is empty. The team that correctly guesses the most people wins!

Example: Gerard Départieu

Clues: *acteur*, *cinéma*, Andie MacDowell, *pas de passeport américain*, and so on.

He Said, She Said: Verbs

So many verbs, so little time and energy. But never fear—you only have to know a handful of verbs to get by nicely. Although you'll have to memorize a few staples, most French verbs are regular and conjugate like clockwork. Who needs all the tenses anyway? Even if you can say it only in the present tense and only in one subject form, you're still likely to be understood though somewhat roughly. As lazy learners, we take pride in saving time, right?

A DIFFERENT DRUM: IRREGULAR VERBS

This section presents irregular verbs. They do not use a recognizable pattern of conjugation. Don't waste time trying to categorize them or trying to understand why they are spelled or spoken the way they are. Just know that they're out there and try to avoid them. (We'll help with that!) Because we are proudly lazy, we'll only ask you to memorize the four most common irregulars. We'll then provide tips for how to combine these irregulars with their more intuitive, regular counterparts.

The Big Four

The four irregular verbs you'll meet in this section will become some of your most useful French tools. At a glance, they might appear to make life difficult because they are irregular, but once you commit them to memory, you'll find they actually facilitate fluency. They are used almost incessantly, not only in everyday speech but in many idiomatic expressions. Idioms, though tricky to learn, are enjoyed by *The Lazy Way* learners because they make us feel particularly French. We'll apprise you of a few common idiomatic expressions as they arise throughout the section and the book.

Avoir (To Have)

This verb is commonly found in idiomatic expressions showing feeling, and it is your ticket to using the past tense. You'll learn more about the past tense in the section "*Hier* (Yesterday): Past Tense" later in this chapter.

j'ai	zhay	I have
tu as	too ah	you have (informal, singular)
il/elle/on a	eel/ell/ohn ah	he/she/one has
nous avons	news ah vahn	we have
vous avez	vews ah vay	you have (formal, plural)
ils/elles ont	eel/ell zahn	they have

Examples:

J'ai un passeport américain.
I have an American passport.

Nous avons deux valises.
We have two suitcases.

Être (To Be)

The verb "to be" is basic to any language. It also is used to tell time.

je suis	zheh swee	I am
tu es	too ay	you are
il/elle/on est	eel/ell/ohn ay	he/she/one is
nous sommes	new sum	we are
vous êtes	vews ette	you are
ils/elles sont	eel/ell zon	they are

Examples:

Je suis étudiant.
I am a student.

Il est deux heures.
It is two o'clock.

Nous sommes perdus.
We are lost.

Aller (To Go)

The verb *aller* puts things in motion. It is found in idioms less frequently than the other three irregular verbs discussed here, but it is your *passeport* to the future tense. You'll learn about the future tense in the section "*Demain* (Tomorrow): Future Tense" later in this chapter.

je vais	zheh vay	I go
tu vas	too vah	you go

One helpful idiom that uses *avoir* demonstrates need. The simple construction *avoir besoin de* goes a long way *en France*. Use it whenever you need it! For example, you can say "*j'ai besoin d'un taxi*" if you need a taxi.

il/elle/on va	eel/ell/ohn vah	he/she/one goes
nous allons	new sah lawn	we go
vous allez	vews ah lay	you go
ils/elles vont	eel/ell vawn	they go

Examples:

Je vais au musée.
I go to the museum.

On va a l'aéroport.
One goes to the airport.

Vous allez à La Tour Eiffel.
You go to the Eiffel Tower.

Faire (To Do or Make)

The verb *faire* has no direct English equivalent. It doubles as both "to do" and "to make." It also is found in numerous idiomatic expressions, which increases its versatility and confuses many French students. For our purposes, remember that *faire* is used in two very common topics of conversation—sports and the weather. (See Chapter 16, *"Entre Amis:* Pleasant Conversation," for guidance in such pleasant chats.)

je fais	zheh fay	I do/make
tu fais	too fay	you do/make
il/elle/on fait	eel/ell/ohn fay	he/she/one does/makes
nous faisons	new fay zon	we do/make

A COMPLETE WASTE OF TIME

The 3 Worst Things To Do with the Verb *Faire*:

1. Memorize all the ways *faire* is used.

2. Stress out about whether to use *avoir, être* or *faire* in idiomatic expressions.

3. Try to pin an English definition on the verb *faire*. Use it to learn it.

vous faites	vew fay	you do/make
ils/elles font	eel/ell fawn	they do/make

Examples:

Je fais du football.
I play soccer.

Il fait beau.
The weather is nice.

Elles font la cuisine.
They are cooking.

LIKE CLOCKWORK: REGULAR VERBS

Phew! You survived the four big irregular verbs. Now you can relax and learn how to handle the easy verbs. All regular verbs come in three groups, and all verbs in one group have the same ending. Once you memorize the conjugations of each group, you can conjugate any regular verb in that group. When in doubt, assume a verb is regular and use it as you would its other group members. If it turns out to be irregular, skip it. Choose a regular verb or a combination of one of the big four irregulars and a regular verb.

-ER   Example: *chercher* (to find)

Remove the *-er* from the infinitive and add the following endings:

Pronoun	ending	sample verb	pronunciation
je	-e	*cherche*	share-sh
tu	-es	*cherches*	share-sh

QUICK **⚫** *PAINLESS*

The pronoun *ce* (meaning this or that) is frequently used in an idiom with the verb *être*. It is conjugated like *il/elle*. The phrase "*C'est ...*" is easy to use when gesturing or answering an inquiry. When eating French food, for example, you might say "*C'est bien*" meaning "That's good."

il/elle/on	-e	*cherche*	share-sh
nous	-ons	*cherchons*	share-shawn
vous	-ez	*cherchez*	share-shay
ils/elles	-ent	*cherchent*	share-sh

-RE   Example: lire (to read)

Remove the *-re* from the infinitive and add the following endings:

Pronoun	Ending	Sample verb	Pronunciation
je	-s	*lis*	lee
tu	-s	*lis*	lee
il/elle/on	-t	*lit*	lee
nous	-sons	*lisons*	lee-zon
vous	-sez	*lisez*	lee-zay
ils/elles	-sent	*lisent*	leez

-IR   Example: choisir (to choose)

Remove the *-ir* from the infinitive and add the following endings:

Pronoun	Ending	Sample verb	Pronunciation
je	-is	*choisis*	shwuh-zee
tu	-is	*choisis*	shwuh-zee
il/elle/on	-it	*choisit*	shwuh-zee
nous	-issons	*choisissons*	shwah-zee-zawn
vous	-issez	*choisissez*	shwah-zee-zay
ils/elles	-issent	*choisissent*	shwauh-zees

DEMAIN (TOMORROW): FUTURE TENSE

Although there is a future tense, we do not suggest memorizing it. Instead, use the verb *aller*, which you already know. Just as you can say, "I am going to [verb]" in English, you can say *aller* + infinitive in French to show future action.

Examples:

Je vais prendre un bus.
I am going to take a bus.

Ils vont faire du jogging.
They are going to go jogging.

Nous allons étudier le français.
We are going to study French.

HIER (YESTERDAY): PAST TENSE

The past tense in French is nearly as simple as the future tense. It's called the *passé composé*. It consists of the verb *avoir* plus the past participle form of the verb. The past participle can easily be created according to the verb groups previously discussed.

Verb group	Ending	Example
-ER	-é	*cherché*
-RE	-u	*lu* (drop the final vowel on the root)
-IR	-i	*choisi*
être		*été*
avoir		*eu*
faire		*fait*

IF YOU'RE SO INCLINED

If you're not a fan of the verb *aller* or are really into conjugating verbs, you can use the present tense to show future intent. Simply tack the appropriate time frame onto your sentence and you're done. For example, you can say "*Je paye le compte demain*" to mean "I am going to pay the bill tomorrow."

Alas, for every rule, there is an exception. In this case, there are 17 exceptions. For 17 specific verbs, you use *être* rather than *avoir* with the past participle to form the *passé composé*. Most of these are irregular verbs having to do with motion. The only one of these rogues you'll frequently tangle with is *aller*. The past participle *allé* follows the appropriate form of *être* in this case. The other 16 are reasonably rare, and it's unnecessary that you memorize them. We recommend that you use *avoir* and simply switch to *être* if your attempt is greeted by a laugh or a confused stare.

Examples:

J'ai fait la cuisine.
I cooked.

Il a lu.
He read.

Vous êtes allé au cinéma.
You went to the movies.

PEUT ÊTRE (MAYBE): CONDITIONAL TENSE

The only time you actually need to employ the conditional tense is when you want something. In this case, you should use the irregular verb *vouloir* (to want) plus the infinitive of your choice. Because the French are sticklers for courtesy, we'll teach *vouloir* only in its conditional form—the only form you should ever use.

je voudrais	zheh voo-dray	I would like
tu voudrais	too voo-dray	you would like

il/elle/on voudrait	eel/ell/ohn voo-dray	he/she/one would like
nous voudrions	new voo-dree-ohn	we would like
vous voudriez	voo voo-dree-ay	you would like
ils/elles voudraient	eel/ell voo-dree-ay	they would like

Examples:

Je voudrais aller à L'Arc de Triomphe.
I would like to go to the Arc de Triomphe.

Nous voudrions trouver un restaurant traditionnel.
We would like to find a traditional restaurant.

Ils voudraient payer avec une carte de crédit.
They would like to pay with a credit card.

Si je vais à Lyon...
If I go to Lyons...

Si vous allez chercher...
If you are going to look for...

S'il fait beau demain...
If it is nice tomorrow...

QUELLE HEURE EST-IL? (WHAT TIME IS IT?): TELLING TIME

As previously noted, the French use the verb *être* to express time. Unpack your French numbers from Chapter 2 and simply say "*Il est...heure(s)*" with the following modifications:

Simply add on the number of minutes past the hour. Use *et* before *quart* (quarter) and *demi(e)* (half). As in English, if it's more than half past an hour, refer to the next hour and subtract the minutes before using *moins*.

QUICK PAINLESS

The French word for "if" is *si*. You can use "if" to make your present tense sentences into conditional statements, thus successfully avoiding the conditional tense.

Use *midi* (noon) and *minuit* (midnight) in lieu of the twelfth hour.

Examples:

Il est une heure.
It is one o'clock.

Il est huit heures dix.
It is ten past eight.

Il est six heures et quart.
It is quarter past six.

Il est cinq heures moins neuf.
It is nine to five.

Il est midi et demi.
It is half past noon.

Il est minuit moins le quart.
It is quarter to midnight.

THE FEW AND THE PROUD: THE ONLY VERBS YOU NEED

One the most important points I have tried to stress throughout this book is simplify, simplify, simplify. In this case, don't learn more verbs than you need. You are better off knowing these crucial ones well than having a shaky grasp of many more.

Verbs You Already Have Learned:

have	*avoir*	irregular
be	*être*	irregular

go	*aller*	irregular
do/make	*faire*	irregular
want	*vouloir*	irregular (cond-tional only!)
seek	*chercher*	regular (-ER)
read	*lire*	regular (-RE)
choose	*chois*	irregular (-IR)

Verbs You Have Not Yet Met:

like	*aimer*	regular (-ER)
need	*avoir besoin de*	idiomatic
rent	*louer*	regular (-ER)
buy	*acheter*	regular (-ER)
find	*trouver*	regular (-ER)
eat	*manger*	regular (-ER)
drink	*boire*	irregular (don't learn)
pay	*payer*	regular (-ER)
take	*prendre*	irregular (don't learn)

IF YOU'RE SO
INCLINED

Practice telling time *en français* by announcing your favorite TV shows. Use any other schedule if you're not much of a couch potato. Say the scheduled time aloud. For example, "Friends *est à huit heures*." ("*Friends* is at eight o'clock.")

The *on* form can be difficult for English speak-
ers. In French, *on* means
one. If, due to a memory
lapse, one can't discuss
what a particular person
(or group of people)
does or needs, one can
talk about what one
does or needs using *on*
just as one would in
English. Very handy!

ACTIVITY: CROSSWORD

I love crossword puzzles. Thanks to Eugene T. Maleska
and Will Shortz I have improved my English vocabulary
immeasurably while having fun. I have created this
French crossword puzzle for you.

Clues

ACROSS

1	Ending for subject tu	prendre
5	On _____ au cin ma.	aller
7	Elle _____ une belle voiture.	avoir
8	Ending for subject il	ER
9	Ending for subject elle	ER
10	This one (pronoun)	masc
11	Ending for subject il	IR
12	Je fais _____ jogging.	article
13	Family for sorti	past participle
14	J'ai _____ d'un billet.	need
17	Plus gentil _____ David	than
18	Ending for past participle	RE
19	Il _____ faire la cuisine.	aimer
21	Family for parlent	ils
22	to find	infinitive

DOWN

1	Past participle	partir
2	Vous _____ ici.	etre
3	Je _____ de le chercher.	decider
4	Ending to make plural	maison
6	Past participle	aller
15	Je _____ heureuse.	etre
16	Ending for subject vous	IR
17	Il est cinq heures et _____.	5:15
20	L'_____ de toilette	water

Crossword

1		2		3	4		5	6
7			8					
		9		10				
				11			12	
13								
			14		15		16	
17					18			
19			20				21	
22								

Chapter

ten

The Cat Is on the Roof: Sentences

"The cat is on the roof" is the first English sentence I ever learned. I've never had occasion to say it, however, except when laughing at its uselessness. In this chapter, you'll learn how to combine everything you know to make complete sentences. You'll also focus on phrases you might actually need—such as "Where's the bathroom?"—rather than silly ones you'll probably never have occasion to say—such as "Le chat est sur le toit." (The cat is on the roof.)

STANDARD ISSUE: BASIC SENTENCES

Forming French sentences is not drastically different from forming their English equivalents. Word order usually is the same, and most sentences translate exactly. The only tricks are adjective placement, gender accord, and elision, all of which you became familiar with in previous sections. How lucky for the lazy!

To form a basic sentence, simply put the pieces together. For example, using the verb *lire* (-RE, regular), which means "to read," you can make the following sentences:

noun + verb
> *Je lis.*
> I read.

noun + verb + object
> *Je lis le livre.*
> I read the book.

noun + verb + adjective + object
> Je lis le livre français.
> I read the French book.

NO-NO'S: NEGATIVE SENTENCES

The glass isn't always half full. At times, you'll need to make negative statements. To make a sentence negative, insert *ne* before the verb and *pas* after it. The effect is similar to that of the English "not." You might need to blend the vowels as you learned to do in Chapter 7, "You Say Potato, I Say *Pomme De Terre*: Nouns." If the sentence has a direct object, you'll also need to change the associated article when making a negative statement. Replace indefinite articles (*un*, *une*, and *des*) with *de*. Definite articles (*le*, *la*, and *les*) are simply removed.

Examples:

> *Je ne lis pas.*
> I do not read.

Je ne lis pas de livres.
I do not read books.

Elle ne fait pas de jogging.
She does not jog.

Vous n'êtes pas des idiots.
You are not idiots.

Advanced Pessimism: More Negative Sentences

When you understand how to use the basic French negative, you can increase its versatility by replacing the word *pas* with any of the following selections:

ne ... rien
nothing

ne ... jamais
never

ne ... plus
no longer

ne ... personne
no one

Examples:

Je ne prends jamais de taxi.
I never take a taxi.

Nous n'aimons personne.
We don't like anybody.

Ils ne font plus de cuisine.
They don't cook anymore.

IF YOU'RE SO INCLINED

Practice your negatives using the different tenses you learned in Chapter 9. In addition to the present negative, try forming past and future negatives. You'll find that, once you say the positive statement, turning it into a negative is easy. Just negate the helper verb. For example, you can say *"je n'ai pas payé"* to say "I did not pay."

DEFINITE OBJECT PRONOUNS

Chapter 7 introduced you to some French pronouns. In that chapter, your task was simply to learn and identify these substitutes. Now let's try using them in sentences. Unlike in English, French pronouns go before the verbs.

Direct (no preposition required in translation)

le, la, les	it, him, her, one, them
me	me
te	you
nous	us
vous	you

Indirect (preposition required in translation)

lui	it, him, her, one
me	me
te	you
nous	us
vous	you
leur	them

Examples:

Je vous aime.
I like you.

Nous ne la parlons pas.
We do not speak it.

Tu lui parles.
You speak to him.

Vous leur offrez une carte.
You offer (to) them a map.

INDEFINITE OBJECT PRONOUNS

The indefinite pronouns *un(s)* and *une(s)* require a slightly different sentence structure in French. To use these handy substitutes, simply place the word *en* before the verb and place the pronoun after it. This is the French way to say "one of those" or "some of those."

Examples:

J'en ai un.
I have one of those.

Il en choisit un.
He chooses one of those.

Nous en avons besoin.
We need some.

MISSING LINKS: CONJUNCTIONS

French conjunctions are much like those found in English. They perform the same task—linking words or phrases within a sentence. You can use them to create more complex sentences by merging simple pieces.

et	and
mais	but
ou	or

Examples:

Je voudrais aller au cinéma et manger du popcorn.
I would like to go to the movies and eat popcorn.

Elle aime le théâtre, mais elle déteste l'opéra.
She likes the theater but she detests the opera.

Ils ont besoin d'un taxi ou d'un bus.
They need a taxi or bus.

SHOW ME THE WAY: PREPOSITIONS

The French use prepositions the same way we do—to show direction within a phrase. Here are a few examples of some French prepositions you'll need to understand and use. Remember, in a worst-case scenario, most prepositions can be replaced by hand gestures!

English	French	Example
at	*à*	*Il va au (à + le) musée à cinq heures.* He is going to the museum at five o'clock.
to	*à*	*Je vais à Paris.* I am going to Paris.
on	*sur*	*Le repas est sur la table.* The meal is on the table.
before	*avant*	*Tu manges avant midi.* You eat before noon.
after	*après*	*Je choisis après toi.* I choose after you.
in	*dans*	*Je dine dans un restaurant.* I dine in a restaurant.

KNOCK, KNOCK: QUESTIONS

Forming a question *en français* is an uncomplicated matter of reversing the subject and verb. If the subject is represented by a pronoun, join the two with a hyphen. In addition, you can start with an interrogative term to ask a specific type of question.

who	*qui*
what	*quoi*
when	*quand*
where	*où*
why	*pourquoi*
how	*comment*

Examples:

Comment allez-vous?
How are you?

Quelle heure est-il?
What time is it?

Où est l'hôtel?
Where is the hotel?

You've forgotten how to invert a sentence. You don't remember the phrase *est-ce que* or any of the interrogative terms. You have questions about questions. What to do? Don't worry. Just lift your voice in an inquisitive tone at the end of a regular sentence. "*On ne fume pas ici?*" ("One does not smoke here?") This works as well in French as in most languages.

YOU'LL THANK YOURSELF LATER

Remember the idiomatic expression *il y a* (there is). You'll hear and use this handy phrase *souvent* (often). For example, if you are peering over the edge of *La Tour Eiffel* and spot a horse below, simply say, "*Il y a un cheval.*" ("There is a horse.")

IN COMMAND: IMPERATIVE

For cultural reasons, we do not recommend that you use the French imperative. You'll be much safer sticking to the conditional of *vouloir* (to want) as you learned in Chapter 7. You'll just need to recognize the imperative when you hear it from the natives. The imperative, or the command form, is simply a verb with no subject to follow. If the imperative has an object, the two will be separated by a dash. You'll note that this tense can have only you (singular or formal/plural) as its implied subject.

Examples:

Continues.
Continue.

Allez à gauche.
Go to the left.

Prenez-la!
Take that!

Activity

Go to your local newsstand and pick out a French magazine or newspaper. Don't worry, we don't expect you to read it all right away! Have some fun translating a section or two. Perhaps you'd like to start with the comics or your horoscope. Have your dictionary on hand because you'll encounter many new words. Pay particular attention to the way the sentences are constructed. Try to spot examples of each type of sentence you just learned.

Become familiar with the phrase *est-ce que*, which is loosely translated as "Is this that?" You can tack it onto the beginning of any French sentence and render it a question. (Put it before the verb but after any interrogatory term.) For example, "*Est-ce que vous l'aimez?*" ("Do you like it?") This construction is an easy way to ask a question without attempting to invert the sentence.

Magazines

L'Officiel (I have a column in this fashion magazine.)

Vogue (*en français*)

Cahiers du Cinéma

Newspapers

Le Figaro

Le Canard

France-Amérique

QUICK  PAINLESS

The French preposition *chez* means "at the home of." *Nous allons chez lui.* (We are going to his home.) *Chez* is also the name of many restaurants: *Chez Louis, Chez Stephan.*

eleven

Savoir Faire: Politeness

The French have a reputation for being difficult. *Mon dieu!* This simply is not true. What is true is that, when beginners speak a foreign language, they sometimes sound rude. Foreigners have limited vocabularies and often must say things in the crudest, most economical terms available. Although *The Lazy Way* embraces a limited vocabulary, it also promotes politeness.

This chapter is filled with shortcuts to becoming the most gracious beginner you can be. If you understand a few key words and phrases and some facts about French culture, you'll be loved by all.

MIND YOUR MANNERS

The rules of politeness in France are similar to the rules of politeness at home. When you need to ask a French person for help or directions or you just want to offer a greeting, keep these tips in mind.

- **Be humble.** No matter how much French you know, you don't know as much as they do. Resign yourself to this

fact and behave with the appropriate amount of humility.

- **Be formal.** The French are sensitive to propriety. Do not ever use the informal *tu* with a French person. Always err on the side of the more formal *vous*. If you get to the point with someone that things become friendly, the person will invite you to use the more familiar construction. I recommend applying this principle to your style of dress as well as to your speech. If you'd like to be treated respectfully, dress with respect. If you plan to visit the great cathedrals of France, for example, do not go out dressed in shorts or a sweat suit.

- **Be grateful.** Always take the time to say a heartfelt *merci beaucoup* when a French person helps you.

DRESSING THE PART

The French love people with whom they can identify. You'll be accepted if you look your best. Dress well—always err on the side of formality (see the preceding section). The French are a stylish lot. Do not wear matching tourist T-shirts or sweat suits. Although these outfits might play in Peoria, they will not go over well in France. I advise friends to wear casual work clothes. Wear basic, neutral colors without flashy patterns. Add a scarf for flair. (This strategy also helps you pack economically—everything will match, and you won't have to pack lots of clothing.) In my experience, this type of wardrobe looks good anywhere on earth.

ACTING THE PART

If you want to do more than just avoid sticking out like a sore thumb, you might want to try to pass as a French person (or at least as an exceptionally cultured American abroad). Frenchness and the absence of it are revealed in subtle ways. Here are some things to keep in mind if you really want to look savvy.

- **Don't drink Coca-Cola** when you stop for refreshments at a cafe. Sure, Coke is beloved around the world, but Americans have a reputation for overdoing it. Instead, have *l'eau minerale* (ask for a brand name—Evian, Perrier, Vittel, Volvic—if you forget the word), a *pastis* (a licorice-flavored aperitif popular in Provence), or something else.

- **Drink wine instead of beer.** The French drink beer, but not like we do in the United States. Wine is the thing to have if you're looking to fit in with the crowd.

- **Drink espresso.** When you order *un café* at *le café*, you'll get an espresso. Many Americans prefer *café au lait* (coffee with milk), which is closer to what most people drink in the United States. Note that *café au lait* is considered a morning drink; resist the urge to order it as your after-dinner coffee.

- **Eat dinner late.** The French do not eat dinner at 6 PM. If you want to be a part of the in crowd, better plan on dinner at 9 PM.

YOU'LL THANK YOURSELF LATER

Remember that *s'il vous plait* is frequently abbreviated *s.v.p.*

Smoking (*le fumeur*) is commonplace in France. People smoke all the time and wherever they like. If smoke bothers you, make a point of sitting outdoors when you can or to look for signs that say *Défense de fumer* (No smoking). Don't comment about it.

MAKING FACES

Friends often wonder whether they'll get anywhere with the French if they smile at them. The stereotype of the scowling French snob filled with *hauteur* is simply not true. I'd say it is true, however, that the French don't smile as much as Americans do. Smiling is fine in moderation. It's always smart to look pleasant when you are asking a question. Smiling can be overdone, however. If you really want to fit in and not be targeted as an absent-minded tourist—especially in a big city like Paris—don't wander around with a vacant grin on your face. (By the way, this is the same advice I'd offer someone asking about any big American city.)

DO UNTO OTHERS

Use common sense. One time, I was in a hotel elevator in New York City with a tourist. When he realized that I lived there, he said something like, "You live here? I don't know how you could exist in so crowded and noisy a place as this." Of course, I was offended. Want to win friends and influence people? Don't complain. Remember what your mother taught you. If you don't have something nice to say, don't say anything at all.

MERCI BEAUCOUP

If you have a limited amount of time in which to learn some French before a trip or if you have a limited mental-storage space, bump these words to the top of the priority list. They are the most important phrases relating to courtesy. Make sure you are able to both speak them and recognize them when they are spoken to you.

Excuse me.	*Pardon.* (as in "excuse me for interrupting")
	Je m'excuse. (more like "I'm sorry" if you step on someone's foot)
Please.	*S'il vous plaît.* (literally, "If it pleases you.")
Thank you.	*Merci.*
Thank you very much.	*Merci beaucoup.*
You're welcome.	*Je vous en prie* or *De rien.* (literally, "It's nothing.")

POLITENESS 102

This is the advanced course of useful tricks. After you've mastered the preceding list, try to make some of the following stick as well. You'll find they're great to fall back on because they can be adjusted for all kinds of situations.

Excuse yourself for interrupting:
"Pardon de vous dérangez, mais ….

Ask whether you can ask a question:
"Est-ce que je peux poser une question, s'il vous plait?"

Take the long route:
"Est-ce que vous pouvez me dire où est le Musée d'Orsay?" not just *"où est?"*

QUICK PAINLESS

Be serious. Don't clown around or try to crack jokes. The joke might not translate. Just stick to being formal and polite and things will go well.

Use *vouloir* conditional:
"Je voudrais acheter deux billets pour l'Opéra, s'il vous plaît." (I would like to buy two tickets for the Opera, please.)

Ask how to say something in French:
"Comment dit-on … en français?"

Addressing Up

If you want to be even more polite when you approach a French native, address him or her properly. Although in more casual America it's fine not to use a form of address, in France, it is preferable. Use either *Madame*, *Mademoiselle*, or *Monsieur*, depending on whom you are addressing. All men should be called *Monsieur*. All women over the age of about 18 should be called *Madame*. Adolescent girls are the only females who should be called *Mademoiselle*.

SLANG AND HUMOROUS EXPRESSIONS

You'll feel more like a native and less like a tourist if you have a few idioms and slang words under your belt. Just think, if someone who didn't speak much English told you he found his friend to be something of a nerd (*un plouc*), wouldn't you be impressed?

Here are some examples of fun, slangy, and idiomatic terms you can use to make your point understood and to really enjoy the language.

un plouc	nerd
le snob	snob

crétin	jerk
truc	thingy (This is a very useful word when you don't know what you really want to say.)
D'accord.	Okay or I agree. (This is another very useful phrase, and it can be employed in many more ways than we use "Okay." You also can use it to say "I understand" and "That's all I needed to know.")
J'ai du blé.	I'm flush. (literally, "I have wheat.")
Je suis fauché.	I'm broke. (literally, "I'm cut down.")
Je suis complete-ment caisée.	I'm exhausted. (literally, "I'm broken down.")

YOU'LL THANK YOURSELF LATER

Note that the French abbreviate salutations, just as we do in English. *Monsieur Desmaison* is written as *M. Desmaison. Madame Balzac* is written as *Mme. Balzac. Mademoiselle Toulouse-Lautrec* is written as *Mlle. Toulouse-Lautrec.*

EXTRA CHARM

If you simply want to be agreeable, remember these words. They can be inserted into conversations or used on their own at any point to make the French think you are a very happy and grateful person. To make things even more great, add *absolument* before these adjectives.

génial	fabulous (*C'est génial!*)
merveilleux (*merveilleuse*)	marvelous
parfait	perfect
formidable	wonderful, impressive

QUICK ■■ PAINLESS

Whenever you can't remember the word for a specific noun, try using the word *truc*. A *truc* is a little thing (literally, "a trick"), but the French use it as we use the word "thingy."

FAUX PAS AMUSANTS

It often is said that we learn from our mistakes. Here are some examples of my friends' mistakes that have made them (and the French people to whom they said them) laugh and learn. You'll certainly return from your trips to France with anecdotes like these.

- My girlfriend, Jennifer, arrived at her hotel and announced "*Je suis une réservation.*" When the hotel staff member said, "*Non,*" she panicked, thinking she'd have nowhere to sleep. She insisted, "*Je suis une réservation.*" He laughed and told her that she had said "I am a reservation." He told her that she might *have* a reservation ("*J'ai une réservation*") but that she, herself, was not a reservation.

- Another friend, Todd, proudly announced to a waiter at the end of a meal, "*Nous sommes finis!*" The waiter laughed and told my friend that he had just said that he and his group were dead. The waiter corrected him with a smile. Instead of "we *are* finished" (which means "we are dead"), he should have said "we *have* finished" ("*nous avons fini*").

- Another friend, Steve, told a family he was eating dinner with that he preferred French bread over American. ("*Je préfere le pain Français.*") When asked why he didn't like American bread, he announced, "*Parce que le pain Américain est plein de préservatifs.*" He was surprised when this got a big laugh. He wondered why everyone was laughing. His French friends reported that he had just told them "Because American bread is filled with condoms." Oops! At least he learned a new vocabulary word. (For the record, preservatives are *agents de conservation*.)

▪ A businessman was in a negotiation in Paris that was going very well. All of a sudden his opposite number started making demands. He was saying, "We demand this, and we demand that." Although startled at first, the businessman realized that the French negotiator was translating the French verb *demander* (which means "to ask") directly into English. Sometimes, speaking a foreign language can help you understand foreigners even when the foreigners are speaking English!

ACTIVITY: IT HAPPENED ONE DAY ...

Use your imagination to think up some scenarios where you would need to be polite. Be creative. If you have a friend who is willing to be your guinea pig, act out some of these scenes with him or her and practice as many of the formal expressions as you can.

IF YOU'RE SO
INCLINED

For more laughs at Americans in France (and all over Europe), rent *National Lampoon's European Vacation* in which the Griswolds blunder their way across the continent. My favorite, of course, is the French section. Use this as an example of what *not* to do.

Bon Voyage: Traveling Basics

The best part of learning French is getting to actually use it, and there's no better place to use your French than in—you guessed it—France! This chapter tells you all you need to know to plan your trip and to get the most out of it. Finding a hotel, renting a car, and buying all kinds of tickets—for the trains, buses, and subway—are made much easier if you know a few key words and sentences.

Most of your plans can be made from your home. I advise that you plan in advance as much as you can to avoid the stress of last-minute language tangles abroad. I also strongly recommend visiting your local French tourist board before you leave. Sometimes you can find great deals and tips there. One of my friends who just visited Paris for the weekend bought a three-day pass to all the major museums and another three-day pass for the subway and buses before she left New York City. (She, of course, had booked her hotel and flight in advance, too.) Because all the details had been handled

YOU'LL THANK YOURSELF LATER

Before you pick up the phone to call a hotel and book a room, write down some of the key vocabulary words you might need: double room, two beds, shower, and so on. This will help prevent you from being at a loss for words when you make your call.

before she left home, she had a very relaxing weekend with no cares (and very few *francs* spent as well)!

GRAND HOTEL: GETTING SETTLED

French hotel rooms come in as many shapes, sizes, and prices as their American counterparts. It's a good idea to know what you want before you book your stay. It's not a given that your hotel room will come equipped with a complete bathroom. Sometimes the shower and toilet are located down the hall; it's best to know exactly what you are getting yourself into.

room	*une chambre*
toilet	*les toilettes*
shower	*la douche*
bathroom	*la salle de bain*
elevator	*l'ascenseur* (m)
single bed	*un lit* or *une place*
double bed	*un lit double*
queen-size bed	*un grand lit*
included	*compris*
breakfast	*le petit déjeuner*
fully booked	*complet*
vacancy	*disponible*
reservation	*une réservation*

Here are some of the sentences I have found most useful in booking hotel rooms alongside their translations.

Je voudrais réserver une chambre avec un lit double et une salle de bain, s'il vous plait.

I'd like to reserve a room with a double bed and a bathroom, please.

Nous arrivons le 12 fevrier et départions le 16 fevrier.

We will be arriving February 12 and leaving February 16.

Est-ce que le petit déjeuner est compris?

Is breakfast included?

Quel est le prix, s'il vous plaît?

How much will that cost? (What is the price, please?)

A Room with a View: Amenities

As romantic as the idea of a tiny attic garret might be when you think of *la vie bohëme* (the life of the bohemian), sometimes you want to splurge. If your wallet allows luxury, make sure your hotel and room come fully equipped with everything you might want.

room service	*le services en chambres*
garage	*le garage*
air conditioning	*la climatisation*
cable television	*le cable*
view	*la vue*
extra	*supplémentaire*
blankets	*des couvertures*
pillows	*des oreillers*
towels	*des serviettes*
hair dryer	*un sëche-cheveux*

IF YOU'RE SO INCLINED

Sorry, king-size fans. Unless you're staying at a luxury hotel, beds bigger than queen-size do not exist.

QUICK 🔘 PAINLESS

Even if you only have one bathroom in your room— as most people do—this term is always plural.

And here's the most important phrase of all:

Pouvez-vous me réveillez a huit heures du matin, s'il vous plaît.

Will you please wake me at eight o'clock in the morning?

Planes, Trains, and Automobiles

The public transportation system in France is a delight. Trains usually are clean, fast, and on time. Airplanes and cars are just as you will find them in America—clean and safe.

If you decide to take a trip via airplane or long-distance train while you are in France, I recommend that you book ahead. The planes, of course, all require reservations and so do many of the trains. Trains such as the TGV (tay-jay-vay), the bullet train that crisscrosses the country, require that you reserve an actual seat. This is best done before you get to the station. Although it can be done at the station, if you hit a busy holiday time, you might end up frustrated as you try to figure out the schedules and make sure the train can accommodate you.

Here are the most important vocabulary words to know before you make your plans.

airport	*aèroport* (m)
airport shuttle bus	*une navette*
taxi	*le taxi*
train	*le train*
train station	*la gare*

ticket	*le billet*
round-trip ticket	*aller et retour*
express	*rapide*
local	*régional*
seat	*un siège*
rental car	*une voiture de location*
automatic transmission	*une transmission automatique*
standard transmission	*une transmission manuelle*
insurance	*l'assurance* (f)
map	*une carte*
highway	*une autoroute*
route	*un itinéraire*

These are the sentences I have found most useful in arranging for travel by train or rental car.

Je voudrais reserver un aller-retour pour Montélimar, s.v.p.

I'd like to reserve a round-trip ticket to Montélimar, please.

Je voudrais partir Samedi et revenir Mardi.

I'd like to leave on Saturday and return on Tuesday.

Est-ce qu'il y a des siège disponible?

Are there seats available?

Nous avons résérvé une voiture avec transmission automatique.

We have reserved a car with an automatic transmission.

QUICK PAINLESS

If you are strapped for cash or just don't have the time and energy to schlep across the ocean, book a trip to Montréal. The capitol of Quèbèc is a delightful francophone city. Naysayers will tell you that it's not real French they're speaking; I'm telling you it is.

Quel est le meilleur itinéraire pour Marseilles?
What is the best route to Marseilles?

The Last Metro: City Transportation

Getting around cities and towns in France is pretty easy.
Of course, it's much less expensive than taking a long-
distance journey, and you don't have to book ahead. You
just jump right on. Buses take change or tickets (conveniently called *les tickets* throughout France).

You need a ticket to get on the subway. You can buy
one either from a clerk or from a machine. My girlfriend,
who is American, finds the machines utterly incompre-
hensible. The metro is the one place she's guaranteed to
speak up and use her wobbly French instead of trying to
read the instructions for a ticket machine. She always
buys from the clerk, which she swears is quicker and less
painful. She advises that other foreigners do this, too.

Big Yellow Taxi: Taking Taxi Cabs

The taxis in France are not yellow; they're just ordinary
cars of any color. Otherwise, they look pretty similar to
what we're used to. There's a box on top of each cab
that, when lit, signifies the car is available. The ride is
measured and priced with a meter that the driver switch-
es on at the beginning of the ride. In most American
cities, you can hail a cab by just sticking out your hand
anywhere you see a taxi going by. In France, however,
there are taxi stands at designated places throughout
the cities. If you need a cab and can't find one, go to the
nearest hotel, civic center (museum, theater, and so on),
or metro stop. There usually will be a taxi stand nearby.

Make sure you know how the prices work—taxis are far more expensive abroad than they are in the United States.

North by Northwest: Directions

If you're like me and every other person I've ever met, no matter how well prepared you are or how keen your sense of direction, you'll get lost at some *pointóso*, and you might have to ask for directions. In my experience, asking for help is one of the things that most scares tourists in France. They fear that their accents will not be up to snuff, that their language skills will fail them, and so on. What they don't think about until they actually have to ask for help usually is the worst part of the problem. They've learned enough French to ask for directions, but they don't know the right words to understand the answers. If you find yourself relying on the kindness of a stranger, make sure you are prepared to benefit from their wisdom. The following words and phrases will help:

If you have special needs, you might want to bring the address of a French agency that can help if you get into a bind. The addresses and phone numbers of several agencies that offer assistance to the disabled can be found in most guide books and on several travelers' Web sites.

English	French	Pronunciation
to the left	*à gauche*	ah-goash
to the right	*à droit*	ah-drwa
straight ahead	*tout droit*	too-drwa
to ascend	*monter*	mawn-teh
to go down	*descendre*	Deh-sahn-dre
under	*sous*	su
at the corner	*au coin*	oh-kwahn
to turn	*tourner*	toor-neh
kilometer	*kilometre*	ki-low-meh-trah

ACTIVITY: PLAN A TRIP

This activity will require a map of Paris. The best kind of map to use is one from a guidebook that highlights the most interesting tourist attractions. Using the map, you will plan a fantasy trip. Imagine that you'll be in Paris for a week, and you want to see the sights inside and outside the city limits.

Imagine that you're staying at the Ritz in *Place Vendôme* and that you want to go to the following places:

Centre Pompidou

L'Arc de Triomphe

Jardin du Luxembourg

Pantheon St. Julien le Pauvre for a concert

Musée d'Orsay

Imagine that you plan to walk to all these sights instead of taking the metro. (You'll use the subway in just a minute.) First, figure out which sights are closest to one another and should be visited together.

Example:

Je visite Le Louvre et puis (and then) *je visite Le Jardin des Tuileries et puis je visite …*

Next figure out exactly how you would get from one site to another.

QUICK ⚏ PAINLESS

The French words for left and right have been incorporated into English. Someone who is gauche (left, as in not right) is considered awkward and clumsy. The French phrase for "to the right" also has been Americanized—adroit. People who are adroit are skilled and talented. (Obviously, lefties were not consulted.)

Example:

Je visite Le Louvre. Après, je prends La Rue de Rivoli tout droit jusqu'au (until) Le Jardin des Tuileries.

Dans Le Métro

Does your travel guide contain a map of the Paris subway system? Most do. And most street maps designed for tourists also feature some key subway stops on them. Get out your map if you have one, and pretend that you're taking the subway to these same destinations.

Example:

Je prends le metro aux Pyramids, change a Gare de L'Est, et arrives a la Porte de Clignancourt pour visiter les Puces (the flea markets).

À Table: Food and Drink

One of the biggest attractions of France is its food and wine. Nowhere else on earth is food so revered and acclaimed as it is in France. If you need proof of this, consider that the French word for food (and kitchen, by the way), *cuisine*, has come to mean good food of any kind—French or otherwise. Also consider the American magazines about food you might enjoy: *Gourmet, Bon Appétit, Saveur*. These French names all are inspired by the glories of French food.

French restaurants and wine can be intimidating. Sure, once you get a bite of that *soufflé* in your mouth you're in heaven, but how should you navigate your way through the menu, the waiters, the wine list, and the markets? Forget the stereotype of the snobby French waiter and the uncouth American customer. Your lazy skills will make you an ace at getting good service and terrific meals.

AT THE RESTAURANT

Because American restaurants are based on the standards set by French restaurants, you will not be surprised by the French dining scene. As in America, there are a wide range of dining

options from casual *cafés* and *bars* to more formal *bistros*, *brasseries*, and *restaurants*.

Types of restaurants include:

Casual: *bars*, *cafés*, bars à vins (*wine bars*), *salons de thé* (tea salons)

Middle: *bistros*, *brasseries*

Formal: *restaurants*

Au Restaurant

Dining out is one of my favorite activities, especially in France. Read these sections carefully before you make your dinner plans.

Réservations

If you are staying at a hotel, you might want to save yourself the trouble and have the concierge make your restaurant reservations for you. If you need to make them yourself, don't sweat it. Making restaurant reservations is a simple exercise in cognate usage: *Je voudrais réserver une table pour deux* (or *trois* or *quatre* or more) *persons à huit heure ce soir.*

Reservations are essential at formal restaurants such as Paul Bocuse in Lyon or Robuchon in Paris. They also are a very good idea at many other restaurants depending on how popular the restaurant is and at what time you'd like to eat. If you want to eat very early by French standards, say 6 PM, it is unlikely you'll need reservations at most places. Check with your guidebooks or hotel staff if you have any questions.

Seating

Do you take a seat or wait to be seated? The answer varies from restaurant to restaurant. As in America, the more formal the establishment, the more likely you are to be seated by a staff member. If you can't tell what to do, see if you can follow another customer's lead. If this is not possible and you must find an economical way of communicating, try catching a waiter's eye and politely saying "*Deux persons, s'il vous plait.*" ("Two people, please.") It doesn't get easier than that.

Menus

Have you ever ordered a *prix fixe* (fixed price) meal in America? This idea—that there is one set price for a pre-determined selection of courses—originated in France. It, as well as the paper it's written on, is called *le menu*. When you are not ordering from the *prix fixe* menu, you are dining *à la carte*. This means you are assembling your courses individually and paying a separate price for each one. The *prix fixe* menu is usually a very good value.

Tipping

In French restaurants, the *service* is always *compris* (included)—by French law—which means you don't have to leave a tip. If you get good service, however, it is customary to leave a token. This usually is just a small percentage of the check, one or two percent in addition to the service charge you've already paid.

Pull Up a Chair

The average French phrase book or language primer provides long lists of words you supposedly need to know to

IF YOU'RE SO
INCLINED

Before you visit France, check out the food columns in the *International Herald Tribune* on the World Wide Web at www.iht.com. Patricia Wells (author of *The Food Lover's Guide to France*) is based in France. *Gourmet* and *Bon Appétit* magazines also have a good web site at www. epicurious.com.

It tastes like chicken!
The French eat some
things that Americans
are squeamish about:
rabbit, frogs' legs,
brains, and so on.
Unless you are willing to
take a culinary gamble,
it might be worth look-
ing up the words for
foods you want to
avoid.

enjoy a French meal. *Learn French The Lazy Way* lets you slack off a bit. Don't bother learning many special wine terms because they all are French anyway. You either already know them, or you aren't a wine snob. It's unrealistic to think you can learn every vocabulary word pertaining to the restaurant world, so we just give you the highlights. Here are the terms we find most easy to remember and most useful. You'll recognize some of them because the French language has donated many words to the vocabulary of global cuisine.

knife	*un couteau*
fork	*une fourchette*
spoon	*une cuillere*
napkin	*une serviette*
plate	*une assiette* (Note: un plat is a course)
glass	*un verre*
bottle of wine	*une bouteille de vin*
maitre d	*maitre d'hôtel*
waiter	*le serveur or la serveuse*
wine steward	*sommelier*
chef	*chef*
breakfast	*le petit déjeuner* (the little lunch)
lunch	*le déjeuner*
dinner	*le diner*

Courses

appetizer	*amuse-bouche*
soup	*soupe*
entree	*premier*
salad	*salade*
cheese	*fromage*
dessert	*dessert*

At Dinner

onion soup	*soupe à l'oignon*
liver pate	*foie gras*
quiche with ham	*quiche lorraine*
salad with tomatoes and anchovies	*salade niçoise*
chicken in wine	*coq au vin*
meat casserole	*cassoulet*
stew	*ragôut*
summer vegetable stew	*ratatouille*
beef in wine	*boeuf bourguignon*
steak and French fries	*steak frîtes*
scalloped potatoes with cheese	*gratin dauphinois*

At the Cafe

coffee	*café*
bread and butter (popular for breakfast)	*tartine*
water	*de l'eau*

Les Plats

QUICK ◼ PAINLESS

In France, an *entree* is an appetizer. This makes more sense really; it is an entry to the meal. What we know as an entree is called the first course. This is followed by the second course, if there is one.

Here are three phrases every phrase book teaches you, but you'll never need to say:

1. I'm hungry.

   J'ai faim. (literally, "I have hunger.")

2. I'm thirsty.

   J'ai soif. (literally, "I have thirst.")

3. I'm drunk.

   Je suis ivre.

If you're hungry, you'll ask where a restaurant is located. ("*Où est un bistro agréable?*"). If you're thirsty, you'll ask where you can find a drink. ("*Je cherche un Coca-Cola.*")

If you have special dietary needs, you should take the time to learn a few key words to let the French know what you can and cannot eat.

vegetarian	*vegetarien*	*Je suis vegetarien.*
diabetic	*diabétique*	*Je suis diabétique.*
kosher	*kascher*	*Je mange kascher.*
low-fat/on a diet	*un régime*	*Je suis un régime.* (I'm on a diet.)

AT THE MARKET

One of the most delightful and increasingly popular ways to enjoy France is to rent an apartment or a house. This enables you to be more of a native and less of a tourist than staying in a hotel does. It also means you'll have a kitchen in which to create your own specialties *du jour*. Even if you don't have your own *chateau* in which

QUICK ⬛ PAINLESS

If you are ravenous but are too tired to use much French, go out and eat like an American. Order *un hamburger* (un am-bourg-err) and *un Coca-Cola*. You also could eat ethnic food—you'll find it easy to order Indian or Italian food.

to cook, you might want to enjoy a roadside *pique-nique* (picnic). These words should come in handy.

The Vegetable Market

France boasts some of the most tempting vegetable markets on the planet. Here are just a few of the most popular items you'll find there. If you don't have time to memorize the names of the vegetables you enjoy most, don't sweat it. At markets in France, you can point to what you want to indicate your needs. *"Je voudrais de celui-ci la et celui-la."* ("I'd like some of these and some of those.")

IF YOU'RE SO
INCLINED

In French restaurants, the salad usually follows the entree.

tomatoes	les tomates
onions	les oignons
garlic	de l'ail
zucchini	les courgettes
asparagus	les asperges
peas	les petits pois
green beans	les haricots verts
potatoes	les pommes de terre
carrots	les carottes
mushrooms	les champignons

Other Stores
Au Boulangerie: At the Bakery

| *croissants* | flaky crescent rolls |
| *brioche* | sweet rolls made from a buttery dough |

baguette	a long thin loaf of bread
pain au chocolat	a croissant in the shape of a square filled with chocolate

À La Charcuterie: At the Deli

saucisson	salami
saucisse	sausage
jambon	ham

À La Boucherie: At the Butcher

le boeuf	beef
le poulet	chicken
le porc	pork
l'agneau	lamb

An understanding of French food terms will help you boost your vocabulary. Look at these words with which you might already be familiar and realize that their meanings can help you outside the kitchen.

sauté—This means to cook over high heat or, literally, to jump (food "jumps" in a hot pan).

frappé—This is another word for milkshake from the verb *frapper* (to beat or strike).

entrée—The *entrée* is the introduction to the meal or an entry to anything you like.

Reading List

Reading cookbooks is an excellent way to get in the mood for French food and to bone up on what's cooking in French restaurants. Our favorites include:

Mastering the Art of French Cooking, Vols. I & II by Julia Child

Bistro Cooking by Patricia Wells

The Food Lover's Guide to France and *The Food Lover's Guide to Paris* by Patricia Wells

A Passion for Potatoes by Lydie Marshall

American Brasserie by Gale Gand and Rick Tramonto

Simple French Food by Richard Olney

Paris Café by Daniel Young

IF YOU'RE SO INCLINED

Make a point of watching The Food Network or renting videos from Julia Child's *The French Chef* series. Your appetite for the language will be stimulated along with your appetite for French food.

ACTIVITY: *SUR LE MENU* (ON THE MENU)

Create your ideal menu. Fill it with foods you'll want to eat in France and memorize what they are. (After you read the exercise at end of the next chapter, you'll be able to come back and fill in the prices.) Be sure to include the *Specialités de la Maison* (house specials) and the *Specialités du Jour* (specials of the day). Create a couple menus and a section of items offered *à la carte*. For example:

In France, there's often a cheese course before dessert. The *fromages* (cheeses) of France have the same names in America. Visit a cheese shop in America so you'll be ready to order them in France: *chèvre* (goat cheese), *brie* (soft, mild cheese), or *roquefort* (strong blue cheese), for example.

Chez Vous

Specialités du jour:
Soupe au pistou
Le Gigot d'agneau

Menu
Soupe à l'oignon
Steak frites
Salade verte
Dessert

À la Carte
Salade d'asperges
Le Rosbif
Poulet rôti

Dessert:
Oeufs à la neige
Crème brulée
Glaces

Prêt à Porter: Shopping

The French are known for their style. Many of the most influential clothing design houses are French: Chanel, Yves St. Laurent, Louis Vuitton, Hermès. The fashion magazines you read in English confirm this, just look at many of their names: Vogue, Elle, Mademoiselle. There's no question that the French are a *chic* lot.

The French are *avant-garde* in other types of design as well, so it might be a good idea to pack an empty bag in your luggage. You might want to *faire du shopping* during your next trip to Paris.

CLOTHING

There are clothing stores of every variety all over France. You can shop in houses of *haute couture* (high fashion) if you have *beaucoup d'argent* (lots of money). There also are many *boutiques* (small shops) such as Agnès B.

If the Shoe Fits: Sizes

French clothing is made in European sizes. Do not be alarmed to discover you've suddenly gone from a size 8 to a size 40. It's just a different numbering system. The best way to understand French sizing if you are buying off the rack is just to look at the clothes. If you are small, take a size 36; if you are larger, take a size 42. Try on the garment and, if it doesn't fit, try to guess your correct size. Trial and error certainly is the best way to go if you have time on your hands and are feeling shy. If you are going to be in a *couture* house such as Chanel (ooh-la-la!), you won't have to worry because the sales people *probablement* will speak English.

If you are shopping for something that can be worn to the store—no bathing suits, please—wear it to the store. Then you can point to the item for which you are shopping without having to ask for it by name.

If you want to make sure you'll be able to communicate your size (*la taille*), memorize the numbers—all sizes are even numbers—that are likely to be in your range:

34	trente-quatre
36	trente-six
38	trente-huit
40	quarante
42	quarante-deux
44	quarante-quatre

Here's some more useful vocabulary:

plus	more (as in *plus grand*)
trop	too (as in *trop cher*)
grand	big
petit	small

IF YOU'RE SO
INCLINED

Visit the big department stores in Paris such as *Printemps* and *La Samaritaine*. They have lovely things to buy and both have nice *cafés*. The latter has a rooftop cafe with a stunning view of the city.

cher, moins cher	expensive, inexpensive
Avez vous une taille plus petite/grande?	Do you have a smaller/ bigger size?
C'est trop petit/grand.	It's too small/big.
C'est un peu cher.	It's a little expensive.
Est-ce qu'il y a des choses moins cheres?	Is there anything less expensive?
la taille	size
les vêtements	garments, clothing
le vestiaire or *le salon d'essayage*	dressing room (room for trying things on)
le mirroir	mirror
chaussures	shoes
chaussettes	socks,
couleur	colors (see Chapter 8 for specific colors)
le shopping	shopping

IF YOU'RE SO INCLINED

Look up the words for the items you'd like to buy before you go shopping. That way, if you need to ask a salesperson for help, you'll have *le mot juste* (the right word) on the tip of your tongue. Notice (and rejoice!) that about half the words you need to know are cognates.

SHOPPING FOR OTHER THINGS

There are many other things you might want to buy in France. If you plan to make any large purchases, you need to know the phrase *"Est-ce que vous expediez en Amérique?"* ("Do you ship to America?") If the shop doesn't offer this service, the owner likely will advise you how to go about it yourself. Make sure you are armed with the right words before you hit the stores.

cookware	*batterie de cuisine*
pottery	*poterie*

furniture	*meubles*
souvenirs	*souvenirs*
toys	*jouets*
jewelry	*bijoux*
books	*livres*
music	*musique*
antiques	*les antiquités*

When you are in France, go to a bookstore (*librairie*) and browse in the children's section. You'll find easy books for French *enfants*. Buy some for yourself. They are a fun way to learn—and your children might learn, too!

AUX PUCES: AT THE FLEA MARKETS

In addition to regular stores, France boasts some of the world's most exciting and unique flea markets and second-hand stores. Check your guidebook for recommendations. If you are in the countryside, find out when market day is. (There usually is one day a week when the village square becomes an open-air market.) Even if it's billed as a vegetable market, you might find stands selling all kinds of things including antiques. If you are in Paris and have time to spare, consider taking the *metro* to *Les Puces*. It's the last stop on the line bound for Porte de Clignancourt. Make sure you go under the overpass and to the left. There you'll find Paris's most famous flea market—streets and streets crowded with antique stores of every kind. Go with the following handy words and phrases in mind and have fun rummaging.

bargain or good deal	*bon marché*
inexpensive or less expensive	*moins cher*
discount or special price	*remise, un prix spécial*

The laws of flea markets in France are the same as those everywhere else in the world. Go prepared to bargain. Part of the flea market culture is bargaining. Ask for a special price or even a reduced price for paying with cash (if the merchant takes credit cards and your purchase is small). Be coy. *"C'est joli, mais comme c'est cher!"* ("Oh, it's so pretty but so expensive!") Play cat and mouse—even if you have to leave and return later—to get the best price.

L'ARGENT

Shopping is great, but you've got to have money. The best way to pay for things, I've found, is to use credit cards wherever they are accepted. When using cash, withdraw it in France from ATM machines. Things have changed dramatically in the last 10 years. The usual routine used to be to change all the money you'd need into traveler's checks before leaving America. Now, ATM machines are so commonplace all around the world that I just change enough cash to get me comfortably from the airport to wherever I am going. I then find an ATM in the center of town. The rates are better at ATM machines, and they are extremely convenient. Make sure you carry lots of coins and paper money in varying bill sizes. You can't ask to pay ten francs for a twenty franc item and then expect the merchant to be happy about breaking a large bill. When you use traveler's checks, you pay a fee to change from dollars into traveler's checks, and then you pay another fee to change from traveler's checks into euros or francs. When you use an ATM

IF YOU'RE SO INCLINED

If you are in Paris and want to take a break, go to Deyrolle on 46 rue du Bac, a famous taxidermy shop. Although you might not want to bring home an ostrich, the shop is worth a look.

The 3 Worst Things to Buy in France:

1. Electrical appliances. They use a different voltage in France than in the United States. You won't be able to use appliances you buy in France.

2. Jeans. America does this best.

3. Fresh food. Although you might want everyone at home to have a taste of that magnificent cheese you found, fresh food is a customs nightmare.

machine, you usually get the rate at which banks trade money between themselves—this is a far better rate than you'll get at a foreign-currency exchange (*bureau de change*).

France is a very safe place if you use your head. Do you usually get robbed in New York City, Los Angeles, San Francisco, or London? It's unlikely if you are street smart. Paris is no more dangerous than these cities. If you keep your money in a safe place, behave wisely, and don't visit dangerous parts of town, there's no reason, in my opinion, to bother with traveler's checks.

If you need cash in France and are not going the ATM route, consider finding the American Express office in the city you are visiting. You will be able to get cash there. Furthermore, the American Express office is filled with people who speak English and can offer other kinds of advice if you are in a bind. I love American Express.

ACTIVITY: CURRENCY

It doesn't help you to know lots of vocabulary for shopping if you don't know how to deal with money. In America, you spend dollars; in France, you spend francs.

Item	Cost in U.S.	French	Cost in France
martini	$7	*martini*	35 francs
leather jacket	$400	*le manteau en cuir*	2000 francs
toothbrush	$2	*la brosse à dents*	10 francs
hotel room	$150	*la chambre d'hôtel*	750 francs

For every dollar you spend in America, you'll spend about five French francs. (Check the exchange rate before you travel; the rate changes slightly every day.)

The preceeding table shows how much certain items cost in America and how much they'd cost in France (these are just approximations and you may find things very different when you take your trip and actually use francs).

When you read the morning paper, spend a moment in the financial section. Look up the exchange rate for the day. When the rate falls, the $20 worth of Francs in your wallet are worth less. When the rate rises, they will buy you more.

Since 1999, the euro has been the currency of France and eight other European countries. The French are a patriotic bunch, however, and still accept francs and even use francs themselves. It will take a while, I suspect, for the euro to really take hold.

IF YOU'RE SO
INCLINED

Even if you are not going to France soon, go to your local bank and exchange $20. Ask for bills as small and as varied as you can get. (Unfortunately, you cannot get foreign coins from an American bank.) Put them in your wallet and, when you buy something, think about how much you'd have to spend for the same item in France.

C'est Le Louvre: Sightseeing

All modesty aside, France is one of the most culturally rich places you'll ever visit. The architecture, museums, theater, cinema, and landscape are bursting at the seams with beauty. Undoubtedly, you'll want to take advantage of it.

This chapter introduces you to some of this bounty and the language you need to access it. Although you could just stumble around the country from painting to park to play, it's better to be able to read the placards, to greet the natives, and to understand some of what you are seeing.

BONJOUR, MONA LISA: MUSEUMS

The museums in France are world class. They feature native and foreign treasures to suit every taste. There are big museums like *Le Louvre*, which houses the *Mona Lisa* and the famous statue of Winged Victory from Samothrace to name just two of its most famous pieces, and *Le Musèe d'Orsay*, where you'll find some of the most prized paintings of the

I urge you to visit some of the smaller museums as well as the big ones. They offer very different experiences that can be immensely rewarding. I love the Victor Hugo museum located on *Place des Vosges*. It is a jewel of a house on a lovely square that you might never otherwise see.

Impressionist period. There's Claude Monet's museum at Giverny, where he painted waterlilies, and the Picasso museum in Paris, which is one of the best collections of the master's work. There's also the Toulouse-Lautrec museum in Albi, the Van Gogh museum in Arles, and the Pompidou Center in Paris, which building itself is a work of art.

If I plan to visit a big museum like the Louvre, I make sure I'm the first person in the door that day (and I try to go off-season if possible, such as in November). Big, famous museums get unbearably crowded as the day goes on. Unless you get there early, you might have to fight to see masterpieces such as the *Mona Lisa*.

I advise against bringing your nice camera to big museums because you usually are forced to check it. You're better off touring the museum for a few hours and then returning to your hotel to pick up your things before you go back out for lunch.

Here are the words from the art world you should know:

museum	*musée*
artist	*artiste* (m & f)
workroom/studio	*atelier*
painting	*peinture*
sculpture	*sculpture*
drawing	*dessin*
contemporary	*contemporain*
Modern	*moderne*

Renaissance	*Renaissance*
Middle Ages	*moyen âges*
medieval	*médieval*

FRENCH ARTISTS

France—and Paris in particular—has always bred and attracted fine artists of all kinds. Here are some of my favorites, whose work you might want to look for while you are visiting:

Les Impressionistes

The Impressionists include Renoir, Manet, and Monet. Their paintings, done at the end of the 1800s, can be found largely at the *Musée d'Orsay*. You also can visit the small town outside Paris called Giverny, where Monet's studio (and waterlily ponds) still stands.

Picasso

Although Picasso was Spanish, he did much of his work in France (in the early 1900s) and has been adopted by the French.

Toulouse-Lautrec

Henri de Toulouse-Lautrec was from Albi, a town in southwestern France that houses a fabulous museum devoted to his paintings and posters. He created many colorful, exuberant posters depicting the bars of Paris night life such as the *Moulin Rouge* and *Folies-Bergëre.* These are reproduced everywhere from magnets to coasters.

IF YOU'RE SO INCLINED

Picasso's museum in Paris is worth the trip as is the *Centre Pompidou,* where you can find some of his paintings.

Rodin

August Rodin was a sculptor who lived in Paris. You'd probably recognize his most famous piece, Le Penseur (The Thinker), a sculpture of a man lost in thought with his chin on his fist. There's a Rodin museum in Paris that is breathtakingly beautiful both for the site and the art.

Encore! Encore!

France has made significant contributions to all the performing arts. Consider these.

Théâtre

In the French performing arts, you'll discover another store of riches. One of the greatest playwrights who ever lived, Molière, was French. His plays such as *The Misanthrope*, *The Imaginary Invalid*, and *Tartuffe* are works of genius still performed widely today. In addition to Molière, France also bred Ionesco, Racine, Sartre, and other acclaimed playwrights. Regrettably, theater in a different language can be very difficult to understand, so you might not want to pursue it.

Musique

Music, happily, transcends language—and there's no want for great music in France.

The *Opéra* in Paris is well worth visiting, whether or not you choose to stay for the show. The building itself is exquisite, and the productions are world class.

A wide range of classical music is available throughout France. Many of the most wonderful

IF YOU'RE SO
INCLINED

Try to catch some French television while you are visiting. You'll notice that many shows are imported from America. If you already know the characters and plots of the shows you see, it'll be that much easier to understand the action.

(and inexpensive) concerts I've been to have been held in churches. There's a great selection of music of every kind, especially in Paris. There are jazz clubs, cabarets, ethnic music events, and more. Guidebooks, hotel concierges, and the local newspaper are the best sources for information about musical events.

Le Cinéma

The French are the biggest film buffs in the world. I know Hollywood is located in America, but I'd argue that it doesn't matter. France has a thriving film scene, and the French have a great appreciation for films from other countries, including Hollywood. *Le cinéma* is taken seriously in France. It is viewed as art as much as entertainment. As I've said previously in this book, one of the best ways to bolster your understanding of the French language and culture is to watch movies. This is easy to do at home, where the movies are subtitled in English, but not so easy in France, where non-French speakers must fend for themselves. When in France, I recommend that you see English-language movies. Go to movies you've already seen that have been dubbed and try to follow along. You'll be amazed at how much you are able to understand. Or go to English-language movies with French subtitles. As you listen to the words, you can read the French translation at the bottom of the screen. This is a marvelous way to pick up some French and to understand how translation

QUICK ☎ PAINLESS

Before you leave on a trip to France, buy and then photocopy the maps you think you'll use most: city maps, maps of the subway systems, and so on. You then can circle the places you plan to visit and make notes on the back without ruining the map or running out of space.

works. You'll be able to discern that some things are lost, some are gained, and translation is rarely as literal as you might hope.

Let the Good Times Roll

We have Toulouse-Lautrec to thank for the image of Paris as a host to naughty cabarets with *risquè* dance and song numbers. Toulouse-Lautrec's posters of women dancing the can-can remain popular 100 years after they were created. At the time, the places he documented were considered to be underworld destinations, worlds of mystery and moral questionability. Today, these cabarets have been cleaned up so tourists can enjoy them. Get your dancing-girl kicks at the *Folies-Bergère* and the *Moulin Rouge*.

Les Bars

The French are big talkers. They love discussing politics, soccer, food, books, philosophy—almost anything, really. One of the most popular activities in France also is popular around the world: chatting with friends over drinks in the local pub.

Bars in France are open very late and are filled with diners at all hours (remember, the French sit down to dinner at nine or ten o'clock) as well as drinkers and talkers.

Au Café

Although the French loiter in bars at night, they loiter in cafes during the day. They are much more likely than Americans to take time out for coffee, a newspaper

If you are trying to pass yourself off as a native, skip the cabaret. Cabarets these days are strictly for the tourists.

break, or a chat with friends during the day—perhaps during *sieste* time in the late afternoon.

A new kind of cafe has recently sprung up in France: the *philocafe* (philosophy cafe). These cafes are devoted to nurturing intense philosophical discussions. Many even have philosophers who are paid to moderate discussions.

On the Town

Paris is renowned for being a beautiful city. The buildings alone—not to mention the works of art and culture inside them—are gorgeous. The parks are well-planned and landscaped; the monuments are impressive and historic. You could visit several cities in France, never set foot inside one of the buildings, and still come away awestruck by the ubiquitous civic beauty.

These are the elements of city and village life you will find most useful.

parks	*parcs*
garden	*jardin*
fountain	*fontaine*
monuments	*monuments*
churches	*eglises*
cathedrals	*cathédrales*
architecture	*architecture*
building	*immeuble*
palace	*palais*
(town) square	*place*

YOU'LL THANK YOURSELF LATER

Visit the Web site salon-magazine.com and go to the Wanderlust section. Look up the articles David Downie has written about Paris. They are wonderful pieces describing the culture and attractions of this great city. (There also are articles about Italy and Amsterdam—he gets around.)

L'HISTOIRE

The history of France is written all over its face. To Americans, things from the 1700s are considered very old. To the French, this is not old at all. The remains of history are evident throughout the country from the prehistoric cave paintings at Lascaux in the southwest to the aqueducts and amphitheaters build by the Romans, from the Gothic cathedrals of the Middle Ages to the Renaissance splendor of *chateaux* such as Versailles, from the Art Nouveau designs of the 1800s to the Pompidou museum of this century.

GÉOGRAPHIE

France's landscape offers something for everyone. It has majestic mountains and fine beaches. There are lush olive-dotted hills in Provence and arid sun-bleached plains in the southwest. Brittany, in the north, is chilly and Atlantic; the Riviera is balmy and glamorous. Alsace-Lorraine, once part of Germany, retains the earmarks of that lusty birthright. Basque country, on the other hand, is more Spanish in flavor because of its proximity to Spain.

Here are some of the regions to which most foreigners are attracted.

■ **Provence.** This region in the south was popularized by Marcel Pagnol's movies and novels of the midcentury and by Peter Mayle's memoirs and novels of the 1980s. It is the sunny land of olives, clear streams, and the licorice-flavored drink *pastis*, and it is a favorite vacation spot for tourists and natives alike.

YOU'LL THANK YOURSELF LATER

If you plan to go abroad, why not read about the history or current events of the nation you will visit?

- **Côte d'Azur.** To the east of Provence lies the Azure Coast. While Provence has a rustic charm, this region exudes glitz, glamour, and tremendous wealth. St. Tropez, Cannes, and Nice are some of the chic cities where you'll find lots of designer clothes, yachts, and movie stars.

- **Normandy.** Made famous by the WWII landing there, Normandy is France's apple country. Don't miss the cider or, if you like it stronger, *calvados*. This is where Jeanne D'Arc was burned at the stake, and it is the site of one of the world's most impressive Gothic cathedrals, in the city of Rouen. On the coastline, you'll find the summer homes of some of the Paris elite. Deauville, for example, where Coco Chanel set up an *atelier*, is a seaside resort town boasting large country houses.

- **Midi-Pyrénées and Rhône-Alpes.** These two regions are very different. The former is in the southwest; the latter is in the east. Both, however, have wonderful ski resorts because both border on mountains—the Pyrenees and the Alps, respectively.

- **Alsace-Lorraine.** Once part of Germany, this area still reflects its heritage. If you are looking for wonderful *brasseries* with traditional, hearty German fare, this is the region to visit.

- **Bordeaux, Bourgogne, and Champagne.** These three regions—located in the southwest, east, and northeast, respectively—are the wine- and, as you could probably tell, champagne-making regions of France.

Many of the vineyards are open to the public for tours and tastings. If you are a wine enthusiast, these areas will delight you.

Géographie de Paris

Paris, like any city, is divided into sections. While New York has the Upper West Side, Chinatown, and Soho (to name a few neighborhoods of a sample city), Paris is divided into 20 sections called *Arrondissements*. When you first look at a map of Paris, you might be confused about how the numbers were selected; they seem to be all over the place. The numbering system actually is quite rational once you realize how it was done. The section on the right bank just by the Louvre is number one. The numbers then spiral out from there in a clockwise fashion. This explains why the second *Arrondissement* is just above it (picture the first *Arrondissement* as starting at 9:00) and the eighth is just to its left.

Just as the regions of France have different personalities, so do the *Arrondissements* of Paris. Here are the highlights of what you'll find:

nº1 This is where the *Louvre*, *Place Vendome* (the square where the Ritz hotel is located), *Le Samaritaine* (a big department store), and *Les Halles* (the old food court) are located.

nº3 In this *Arrondissement*, you'll find part of *Le Marais*, a neighborhood once known for its heavy Jewish population. This is a very residential area. You'll also find craftsmen such as silversmiths and leatherworkers in this neighborhood. Don't miss the Picasso museum here.

n°4 The rest of *Le Marais* is in the fourth *Arrondissement*. This currently is where the gay night life is centered. *Place des Vosges* is a lovely square that used to be called *Place Royale*. Victor Hugo, the novelist, used to live here. *Ile St. Louis* and part of *Ile de la Citè*, the two islands in the middle of the River Seine, are in this *Arrondissement*, as is *Notre Dame*.

n°5 Crossing the river to the *Rive Gauche* (the Left Bank), the fifth *Arrondissement* is the home of the *Quartier Latin* (the Latin Quarter) and *La Sorbonne* (the famous university). This is the bohemian part of town where Gertrude Stein and her friends spent a lot of time.

n°6 This is the posh part of the *Rive Gauche*. It is home to art galleries, bookstores, and antique stores. The area often is called *St. Germain*.

n°7 This is a residential area that is still chic and has very old money. This is where many government buildings (*ministeres*) are located. Napoleon is buried here in *Les Invalides*. And don't miss the Eiffel Tower.

n°8 *Champs-Elysèes* is the home of one of the grandest boulevards in the world, which begins at *Place de la Concorde* and ends at *l'Arc de Triomphe*. This is the Fifth Avenue of Paris and features many restaurants, cafes, and shops.

QUICK ☺ PAINLESS

"n°" is the French abbreviation for "numéro" meaning "number."

n°9   *L'Opèra* is located in the ninth *Arrondissement*, as is *Le Printemps*, one of Paris's great department stores. This is where *Folies-Bergère*, the famous cabaret, is found.

n°11   *Bastille* and *Republic* are big, historic squares. They have been sites of political demonstrations throughout history as well as in the present.

n°14   *Montparnasse* is the part of town where artists such as Picasso used to live.

n°18   *Monmartre* is the section of town that is home to *Sacre Coeur* (Sacred Heart Church) and is another place once populated with artists. This very hilly section of Paris affords a good view of the city and an adventure if you feel like taking your rental car up the hill.

n°20   *Père Lachaise*, a cemetery, is the final resting place of many famous people. Bring flowers for Jim Morrison's grave.

ACTIVITY: THE HISTORY CHANNEL

With a fellow French student, create short multiple-choice tests using famous French landmarks and quiz each other. Start with these examples.

1. *La Rive* _____ is the Left Bank of the _____.

2. *La* _____ *d'Azur* is the playground of the rich and famous.

3. Napoleon was exiled to the French isle of _____.

A COMPLETE WASTE OF TIME

Paris does have a Chinatown, but why visit it when there are so many unique sites to see?

4. The movie *The French Connection* was set in the lusty port city of _____.

5. Two of France's most famous cathedrals are located in _____ and _____.

6. Monet painted waterlilies at _____.

7. We are going wine tasting in _____ and skiing in _____.

8. Louis XIV made his home at _____.

    A.   Gauche

    B.   Côte

    C.   Corse

    D.   Marseilles

    E.   Chartres

    F.   Reims

    G.   Giverny

    H.   Bordeaux

    I.   Biarritz

    J.   Versailles

My favorite map of Paris is called *Paris Par Arrondissement*. (*Arrondissements* are the numbered sections of the city.) It is a small red book that can be purchased at your local news kiosk in Paris or at any French bookstore in the U.S. It shows every street, large and small, and is invaluable.

Chapter

sixteen

Entre Amis: Pleasant Conversation

Now that you've mastered the French basics, it's time to put them to work in the art of conversation. In this chapter, you'll learn how to discuss some common topics, and you'll find tips for handling conversation in general. Most importantly, remember to relax and enjoy yourself. The French tend to speak quickly, so if you need someone to speak more slowly, simply smile and say, *"Plus lentement, s'il vous plaît."* ("More slowly, please.") or *"Répétez, s'il vous plaît."* ("Repeat, please.") This is a rare instance in which you can use the imperative without offending someone.

RAIN OR SHINE: THE WEATHER

The French use the verb *faire* to discuss the weather. The noun for weather is *le temps*, which usually is replaced by the pronoun *il*. *"Quel temps fait-il?"* ("What is the weather (like)?") Here are some possible responses:

Il fait beau.	It's nice.
Il fait soleil.	It's sunny.
Il fait chaud.	It's hot.
Il fait mauvais.	It's bad.
Il fait froid.	It's cold.
Il fait du vent.	It's windy.
Il pleut.	It's raining.
Il neige.	It's snowing.

Paris in the Springtime: Seasons

France has four seasons just like most English-speaking areas. The following are the French words for the seasons. Use them with the preposition *en* (except for spring, which requires the use of *au*). Note that the French do not capitalize the names of the seasons as we do in English.

English	French	Pronunication
spring	*le printemps*	le prehn-tomp
summer	*l'été*	leh-tay
autumn	*l'automne*	low-tuhm
winter	*l'hiver*	lee-vare

Examples:

Au printemps, il pleut.	In spring, it rains.
Je vais en France en automne.	I am going to France in autumn.
Il ne neige jamais en été.	It never snows in summer.

The French use the Celsius scale to tell temperature. The word for degrees is *degr*é, a close cognate. To convert Celsius to Fahrenheit, multiply the Celsius temperature by 1.8, then add 32. This will give you a Fahrenheit temperature you recognize.

MAKING A DATE: THE CALENDAR

Dates also are written with a French twist. *Par example*, the 14th of July is Bastille Day in France, a holiday similar to the American Independence Day. You will learn how to celebrate Bastille Day in Chapter 18, *"Les Fêtes*: Celebrations."* For now, let's try writing this date in French:

> *14 juillet 1998*
>
> *le quatorze juillet 1998*

These are both correct ways to write July 14, 1998 *en français*.

As with the seasons, the French do not capitalize the months. In French, use the preposition *en* to say "in the month of." Here are the French months:

English	French	Pronunciation
January	*janvier*	zhahn-vee-ay
February	*février*	feh-vree-ay
March	*mars*	mahrs
April	*avril*	ahv-reel
May	*mai*	meh
June	*juin*	zhoo-ehn
July	*juillet*	zhwee-ay
August	*août*	oo
September	*septembre*	sehp-tahm-bruh
October	*octobre*	ock-tow-bruh
November	*novembre*	no-vahm-bruh
December	*décembre*	day-sahm-bruh

IF YOU'RE SO INCLINED

Start reading a French weather report regularly. Refer to the newspaper you bought in Chapter 10, "The Cat is on the Roof: Making Sentences." The weather report uses nouns to describe the local weather: ***soleil*** means sun, ***couvert*** means cloudy, ***pluies*** means rain, *neige* means snow, ***orages*** means storms. This also is a good time to practice your Celsius conversion skills!

Practice saying dates in French using the birthdays of your family members or close friends. Announce the name and then say the date of the corresponding birthday. You might say, for example, "*Ma sœur, son anniversaire est le neuf novembre.*" ("My sister's birthday is the ninth of November.")

QUEL ÉTAGE? (WHICH FLOOR?): OTHER NUMBERS

Although the French simply use cardinal numbers to refer to dates (as previously shown), you still might want to specify one of something using ordinal numbers. To say the first, second, third, and so on in French, simply change the ending of the number to *ième* (except in the case of the first, which is *le premier*).

Examples:

French	Abbreviation	English
le premier or la première	1er or 1ère	the first
le quatrième	4è or 4ème	the fourth
le onzième	11è or 11ème	the eleventh
le dix-huitième	18è or 18ème	the eighteenth

TAKING NAMES: INTRODUCTIONS

When you meet a new *ami*, you'll need to know how to introduce yourself and your companions. If you'd rather not point at yourself and grunt, "Tarzan," use the verb *s'appeler* (to call). This is called a reflexive verb because the subject and the object are the same. (The action described by the verb *reflects* on the verb's subject.) "*Je m'appelle Christophe.*" ("I call myself Christophe." or "My name is Christophe.") The *s'* stands for *se*, the reflexive pronoun, and the verb *appeler* is a regular -ER group member (except that the "l" is doubled in conjugation.)

Reflexive Pronouns

me	myself
te	yourself
se	himself, herself, oneself, themselves
nous	ourselves
vous	yourself, yourselves

Examples:

Je m'appelle Jean.	My name is Jean.
Il s'appelle Marc.	His name is Marc.
Elles s'appellent Marie et Suzette.	Their names are Marie and Suzette.

YOU'LL THANK YOURSELF LATER

Remember that, in France, the metric system is king. Road distances are measured in kilometers and speeds are in kilometers per hour. A kilometer equals 0.62 miles.

If you want to learn more about reflexive verbs, here are a few more you might find useful. If you do not want to get involved with these verbs, skip them. Don't worry about memorizing lists of reflexive verbs. Just memorize how to use *s'appeler* and pretend it's an idiom. If you are truly lazy, however, you can skip learning these words.

se coucher	to go to bed
se réveiller	to wake up
se baigner	to bathe
se dépêcher	to hurry
se promener	to take a walk
se tromper	to make a mistake

PHONE NUMBERS AND ADDRESSES

French phone numbers and zip codes use the basic numbers you learned in chapter two, but they have a slightly different format than their American counterparts. Street addresses also differ from American street addresses.

Phone Numbers

Speaking on the phone is difficult, but it can sometimes look easy compared to dialing the phone in a foreign country. Here are some helpful details on getting connected to the right number.

Calling from America:

011-33-1-xx-xx-xx-xx

011 is the prefix you dial for all international calls.

33 is the country code for France.

1 is the regional code for Paris.

When you have dialed 011-33-1, dial the phone number, represented above as xx-xx-xx-xx. All French phone numbers have eight digits.

Calling Within France:

01-xx-xx-xx-xx

Dial a regional code, and then the phone number.

Regional Codes:

01   Paris

02   NW

When you are listening to someone give you directions, remember that he or she likely will be speaking in the imperative tense. ("Go to the corner. Turn right.")

03 NE

04 SE

05 SW

06 Cellular

On the Horn: Telephone Manners

The French word for phone is *le téléphone*, a cognate. This word also functions as a verb, *téléphoner* (-ER, regular). The following are some snippets of French phone chatter for you to learn.

Allô.	Hello.
Est-ce que Philippe est là?	Is Philippe there?
C'est Sophie.	It's Sophie.
Je voudrais parler à Georges, s'il vous plaît.	I would like to talk to Georges, please.
Ne quittez pas.	Hold on. (Literally, "Don't hang up.")
Un moment.	Just a moment.
Il n'est pas là.	He is not in.
Je voudrais laisser un message, s'il vous plaît.	I would like to leave a message, please.
Je vais rappeler plus tard.	I'll call back later.
Merci, au revoir.	Thank you, goodbye.

Addresses

Here are the addresses of two popular French tourist spots. Notice the word order and how they are written:

QUICK ☞ PAINLESS

In general, reflexive verbs (such as "to bathe") have the same subject and object. You do usally bathe yourself?

Fauchon (a restaurant)
26, Place de la Madeleine
75008 Paris

Musée du Louvre (a museum)
34-36, quai de Louvre
75001 Paris

ARE YOU GAME? SPORTS TALK

A favorite topic of conversation in almost any country is sports. French people are particularly interested in soccer (*le football*), bicycling (*le vélo*), rugby (*le rugby*), and auto racing (*les courses automobiles*). Remember, you use the verb *faire* to discuss most sports.

Faites-vous du vélo?	Do you bicycle?
Oui, je fait du vélo souvent.	Yes, I bicycle often.
Aimez-vous le football?	Do you like soccer?
Non, mais, j'aime le football américain.	No, but I like football.

COME PLAY WITH ME: HOBBIES

Obviously, there are many things to talk about in France besides sports and the weather. The following are a few other terms you might use to discuss topics that interest you. Do not worry about memorizing this vocabulary. You can always look up an activity in your *dictionnaire* if the urge suddenly strikes you in France. If a word here describes something you enjoy, however, you might want to memorize it.

YOU'LL THANK YOURSELF LATER

If you want to talk about football in Paris, remember that the French word *football* means soccer. To talk about American football, you need to know the term *football américain*.

beach	*la plage*
pool	*la piscine*
to swim	*nager* (-ER, regular)
golf course	*le parcours*
disco	*le discothèque*
to dance	*danser*
play cards	*jouer aux cartes*
mountain	*la montagne*
park	*le parc*

ACTIVITY: ROLE PLAY

This activity is fun to try with other students of French. Choose a character from French culture or history to play for a few hours. Be a king, a conqueror, a writer, or a performer at the dinner table or during a long car trip. Have your *ami* interview you or take on a persona as well. Try to imagine how your characters would interact. This is a fun way to experiment with your budding French conversation skills.

QUICK ⬛ PAINLESS

There are plenty of brand names you can use when talking in France. For instance, you don't ever need to say "rental car," you can just say that the car is from (or that you are looking for the office of) Hertz, Avis, or EuropeCar.

Chapter seventeen

Trouble in Paradise: Problem Solving

Although we hope your every moment in France will be pleasant, there's always the possibility that something could go wrong. Whether it's your language skills, your health, or your car that breaks down while abroad, after reading this chapter, you'll be prepared to handle the situation. If you're a diehard optimist, you might want to skip this chapter and assume the best. A pessimist might memorize it. Wherever you fall between these two extremes, you'll know you can refer to this chapter should a problem arise while you're *en France.*

GREEK TO ME: WHEN YOU DON'T UNDERSTAND

Despite your lazy yet effective strategies for handling conversations, you will not always understand everything a French person says to you. When this happens, use the following

phrases to ask for further clarification. Keep them handy so you can easily reach for them in times of confusion.

Plus lentement, s'il vous plaît.	More slowly, please.
Répétez, s'il vous plaît.	Repeat that, please.
Parlez-vous anglais?	Do you speak English?
Je parle le français seulement un peu.	I only speak a little French.
Comment dit-on …?	How does one say …?
Qu'est que c'est?	What is this/that?
Je ne comprends pas.	I don't understand.

À VOTRE SANTÉ: YOUR HEALTH

Suppose you forget how to convert Celsius to Fahrenheit and find yourself in a snowstorm without a warm coat. You'll probably catch a cold (*un rhume*). If you get really sick, you might need to go to the hospital (*l'hôpital*) or to see a doctor (*le docteur*). At the very least, you'll want to buy a box of tissues from the drugstore without incident. In French pharmacies, many items are behind the counter and need to be requested by name. Here are a few of the items you might need:

À La Pharmacie

les mouchoirs	tissues (Kleenexes)
le papier hygiénique	toilet paper
l'aspirine (f)	aspirin
les serviettes hygiéniques	sanitary pads

le bandage	bandage
le pansement adhésif	Band-Aid
le médicament pour le rhume	cold medicine
l'huile solaire	suntan lotion
le savon	soap
la brosse à dents	toothbrush
la dentifrice	toothpaste
le shampooing	shampoo

Bag of Bones: Your Body

If you have a pain somewhere, you'll need to tell the doctor where it hurts. You can either point to the affected area and groan, or you can use one of the following terms for body parts. Simply say, "*J'ai mal* à [insert body part here]" to indicate where it hurts.

la tête	head
le cou	neck
la gorge	throat
l'oreille	ear
l'œil	eye
les yeux	eyes
la dent	tooth
le nez	nose
la jambe	leg
le bras	arm
l'estomac	stomach
le pied	foot

QUICK ⬤ PAINLESS

Rather than memorizing lists of types of doctors, use the body parts to create them. The French word for doctor is *le docteur*. Add *pour* and make your own specialist. If you need to see a podiatrist, try "*J'ai besoin d'un docteur pour les pieds.*" ("I need a foot doctor.") *Voilà*!

la main	hand
la cœur	heart
le dos	back
les genoux	knees

Problems

Sometimes you need to get more specific about what's wrong. Here are some of the most common problems you may have and might need to communicate to someone else.

General

Fiévre	fever
rhume	cold
migraine	migraine
blessé	cut, wounded

Specific

Diabète	diabetes
crise cardiaque	heart attack
grippe	flu
infection	infection

911: REAL EMERGENCIES

If you experience a medical emergency, you'll probably resort to shouting. Here are a few things you can yell:

Au secours!	Help!
A l'aide!	Help!
Docteur!	Doctor!

Although there's no French equivalent for 911, nearly every French phone has the numbers for the police and fire departments listed on it. If you have a serious crisis, run for a phone and you'll see the numbers.

The Breakdown Lane: Car Problems

Although I won't cover all car problems here (this is not an auto manual), I will teach you a few terms. I don't recommend memorizing them unless you're a car nut, but if you're going to be driving in France, you ought to at least know how to get gas and a few other basic terms.

la voiture	car
conduire	to drive
un pneu crevé	flat tire
changer une roue	to change a tire
tomber en panne	to break down
tomber en panne d'essence	to run out of gas
un garage	garage
une station-service	gas station
le capot	hood
le coffre	trunk
la batterie	battery
l'essence (f)	gasoline
Le plein, s'il vous plaît.	Fill it up, please.

YOU'LL THANK YOURSELF LATER

Memorize the French words for right, *droit*, and left, *gauche*. These will prove very useful. Like most adjectives, they follow the nouns they modify. For example, "*J'ai mal à mon pied droit.*" ("I have pain in my right foot.")

l'huile (f)	oil
l'antigel (m)	antifreeze
les clefs (f)	keys
Nous sommes perdus!	We are lost!

Directions

au nord	North
au sud	South
à l'est	East
à l'ouest	West
a gauche	to the left
a droit	to the right
tout droit	straight

Lost and Found

Hopefully, you won't misplace any of your important belongings while in France, but it could happen. Perhaps you'll be concentrating on your new language skills and mislay your wallet. Or maybe your luggage won't make the trip with you. Everyone has survived a few of these unfortunate events while traveling. With the following tips, you will, too.

If you lose your passport (*le passeport*) in France, you'll need to go to the American Embassy to get another one. Here's the address in Paris:

2 Avenue Gabriel
75382 Paris
Téléphone: [33] (1) 42 96 12 02, 42 61 80 75

If your wallet (*la portefeuille*) has disappeared, let's hope you had the foresight to get an American Express card. If so, you can go to the nearest American Express bureau for help. If you are not a card member, try your hotel desk for assistance. If the folks there can't help you, they certainly can point you in the direction of someone who can.

Finally, if your luggage (*les bagages*) does not arrive at your destination when you do, simply go to the customer service facility at the airport. You'll need to fill out some forms so the airline can send your bags to you when they are found. Don't get upset—this is an excellent excuse to go shopping in Paris!

ACTIVITY: I'M GOING ON A PICNIC AND I'M TAKING ...

Play the word/memory game you may have enjoyed as a child on long car trips. The first player starts, "I'm going on a picnic and I'm taking a [noun];" or in this case "Je fais un pique-nique et je prends un(e) [nom]."Pick the noun of your choice, for instance, "Je fais un pique-nique et je prends une bouteille de vin [a bottle of wine]." The next player must then repeat your noun and add one of his or her own. For instance, "Je fais un pique-nique et je prends une bouteille de vin et un lit [a bed]." And so on. It doesn't matter if the nouns make sense or not. As long as you are repeating and understanding them, your vocabulary will improve. For an added challenge, try adding the nouns in alphabetical order.

QUICK ⬤ PAINLESS

Chapter 6, which covered cognates, discussed how you can use brand names in lieu of elusive vocabulary words. Here are a few pharmaceutical brand names the French will recognize: Kleenex, Tampax, and Advil.

Les Fêtes: Célébrations

The French find more reasons to celebrate than we do. This predominantly Catholic country still celebrates saints' days left and right, despite its insistence on the separation of church and state. (*Vive la révolution!*) Therefore, it's important to know what the holidays are. (We can't list them all here, so check your calendar before you head to France. You don't want to find on a day you set aside for shopping that all the stores are closed.) If you find you cross paths with a holiday, you'll delight in the festivities you find.

WINTER

Christmas is celebrated in France much as it is in America. Although America celebrates predominantly on December 25, most French choose December 24 as the day of their big celebration. My family, for example, attends Mass at around 10 PM on Christmas Eve. (We used to go to Midnight Mass, but that just became too late for us.) We then return home for a late supper capped off with the traditional *bouche de noel*. (This translates literally as "Christmas log," a cake in the shape

of a log.) We exchange gifts and end up going to bed around 3 AM.

Oui, Virginie, il y a vraiment un Pére Noël. (Yes, Virginie, there really is a Santa Claus.) In France, we call him *Pére Noël* (Father Christmas). In France, as in America, *les enfants* awaken on Christmas morning to find that *Pére Noël* has left goodies for them under the tree.

Christmas Words

Merry Christmas	*Joyeux Noël*
Christmas tree	*arbre de Noël*
presents	*cadeaux*
candles	*bougies*
angels	*anges*
ornaments	*décorations*
wreath	*couronne*
stars	*étoiles*
nativity scene	*une créche*
fireplace	*une cheminée*

Hanukkah

Hanukkah is celebrated in France just as it is in America. If you are Jewish, you don't have to learn as much vocabulary as you would for Christmas because Hebrew is the language of the Jewish holidays. The Hanukkah terms are mostly the same: menorahs, dreidels, the whole nine yards. Hanukkah (and all the Jewish holidays—les *fêtes Hébraiques*), you will find, is not as widely celebrated in France as in America because there's a smaller Jewish population. Most Jews, you should note, live in Paris. If you plan to celebrate Jewish holidays while in France, it is best to be in Paris or with a Jewish family.

New Year's Day (*Le Nouvel An*)

Just like you, the French like to ring in the new year with good cheer. They attend parties, toast with champagne, wish each other good tidings. Note that New Year's Eve also is the feast of Saint Sylvestre; you might also hear reference to him. Here are the essential terms to know if you are celebrating this occasion in France.

New Year Words

Happy New Year!	*Bonne Année!*
to celebrate the new year	*Faire le réveillon de nouvel an*
to wish	*souhaiter* (as in "*Je vous souhaite [sueette] une bonne année.*")
to make New Year's resolutions	*Prendre les résolutions de nouvelle année*

Les Montagnes (The Mountains)

In the wintertime, many French people take their holidays in the mountainous regions of the country. They visit the Alps (*les Alps*) on the border of Switzerland and

IF YOU'RE SO
INCLINED

If you are Jewish or are interested in exploring Jewish culture at Passover or any other time of the year, visit the section of Paris called *Le Marais*. This is the old Jewish part of the city where you can find Jewish bakeries serving traditional Jewish foods such as rugelach, hammanaschen, and challah.

the *Pyrénées* on the border of Spain. There they go skiing and play in the snow. If you like snowy frolics and seasonal glamour, you might want to visit these resort areas as well.

Snow Words

skiing	*faire du ski*
snow	*la neige*
winter house	*chalet*
snowboarding	*le snowboarding*
to go ice skating	*faire du patin*

SPRING

Easter (*La Pâques*) marks the end of Lent (Pâques le Carême). It is the most holy day of the Christian year, and the celebration of the holiday is more religious than others such as Christmas.

Easter Words

Easter egg	*œuf de la Pâques*
to hunt	*chasser*
Easter bunny	*lapin de la Pâques*
ham	*jambon* (the traditional Easter food)

May Day (*La Fête du Travaille*)

In America, Labor Day is at the end of the summer. The French labor day, however, is at the beginning of summer. May 1st also marks the start of spring, so it's heralded with parties and fairs usually held, at last, *en plein air* (outside).

May 8th—*La Libération*

May 8th marks the day Paris was liberated at the end of World War II. Paris, as you might know, was occupied by Germany during the War. May 8, 1945 was the day Allied troops marched into town and freed Paris from the Nazis. There are celebrations in the streets and most shops are closed.

Cannes

The Cannes festival is one of the world's premier film festivals. During the festival, Cannes and Nice are filled with celebrities of every nationality. If you like to see and be seen, visit the festival. Make sure you book your hotel in advance because rooms fill up quickly and are *très cher*.

Film Words

celebrities	*célébrites*
films	*films*
director	*metteur en scène*
awards	*prix*
first prize at the Cannes festival	*Palm d'Or* (Golden Palm)

SUMMER

The *Tour de France* is the Boston Marathon of bicycle races. All the best cyclists from around the world

IF YOU'RE SO INCLINED

Brush up on the American celebrities the French love before you plan a trip to Cannes. The French adore *auteurs* such as Woody Allen, Martin Scorsese, and Francis Ford Coppola. And yes, it's true, the French really are in love with Jerry Lewis. If you want to score points with them, get to know his *œuvre*.

Bastille Day is just as crazy and crowded as our Fourth of July. If you like big celebrations, I recommend being in Paris for this one.

converge on France at the end of June and the beginning of July to compete in the world's most grueling and rewarding cycling competition. The competition begins in a different country every year, but it always finishes in Paris. The race is over 2,500 miles long and covers every kind of terrain imaginable from flat stretches to mountainous routes. The winner of the race is awarded a yellow jersey (*le maillot jaune*) and, of course, a cash prize. The race is a very big deal in France. If you are a cycling enthusiast, it is worth the trip.

July 14th—Bastille Day (*Le Quatorze Juillet*)

Bastille Day is the French day of independence. On July 14, 1789, the Bastille, a jail that housed political prisoners, was opened and the inmates were released. It marked the end of the tyranny of the elite. It really is just like the Fourth of July in America with fairs, parades, and fireworks. If you are claustrophobic or hate crowds, however, plan to be out of town on this day.

Revolution Words

Liberté, Egalité, Fraternité	Liberty, Equality, Brotherhood (the motto of the French Revolution)
"La Marseillaise"	The French national anthem

La Bastille	An old Parisian prison so notorious that a part of town was named for it

Août (August)

The French take their summer holidays in August. This is due in large part to the fact that the feast of the Assumption (the assumption of the Virgin Mary into heaven) is celebrated on August 15 (*le quinze Août*). If you are traveling in France any time in August, you'll notice that many restaurants and shops are closed all month while the patrons are on vacation.

In August, the French take to the countryside. They go to their summer homes outside the cities and sometimes travel abroad. You also might want to travel in the countryside at this time of year because it can be very hot and humid, especially in urban areas.

Vacation Words

vacations	*les vacances*
mountains	*montagnes*
hiking	*promenade*
beach	*plage*
sand	*sable*
swimming	*natation*
pool	*piscine*
picnic	*pique-nique*
summer house	*maison de vacances*

IF YOU'RE SO
INCLINED

Rent the movie *Casablanca* and pay close attention to the scene in which Victor Laszlo commandeers the band at Rick's and leads the crowd in a rousing rendition of "La Marseillaise," drowning out the German contingent that had started singing "Deutschland, Deutschland, Uber Alles." You'll probably be able to pick out some of the words, and you'll at least be able to hum along at the end.

Words for Dates

SEASONS	SAISONS			Saturday	samedi
winter	hiver			**MONTHS**	***LES MOIS***
spring	printemps			January	janvier
summer	été			February	février
autumn	automne			March	mars
DAYS OF THE WEEK	***LES JOURS DE LA SEMAINE***			April	avril
				June	juin
Sunday	Dimanche			July	juillet
Monday	lundi			August	août
Tuesday	mardi			September	septembre
Wednesday	mercredi			October	octobre
Thursday	jeudi			November	novembre
Friday	vendredi			December	décembre

When planning your trip and when you are in France, the words in the preceeding table will be very useful.

WHEN TO TRAVEL?

The best time to travel in France, I feel, is off-season. I love returning to Paris in months such as November and March because there are very few tourists and the airfares and hotel rates are low. If you try to see the Mona Lisa in the Louvre in July, you'll have to stand in a long line and view her with a crowd. If you go in November, you'll be able to have a lovely, private *tête-à-tête* with the *Mademoiselle*.

If you are visiting the south of France, however, summer really is divine despite the crowds. Provence, which was popularized by Peter Mayle's best-selling books (see Appendix b), is quite cold and windy in the winter. In summer, it is sunny, warm, and could not be more pleasant. I love Provence in summer. Places such as Cannes and St. Tropez are crazy in the summer months. The traffic is unbearable, but still these are places best visited in nice weather. I recommend to friends that they visit the *Cote d'Azur* in May or September—just slightly off-season to avoid the throngs in thongs but still enjoy the weather.

ACTIVITY: *LA FÊTE*

Throw yourself a party! You deserve it. You've just about finished your lazy course, so it's time to reap your rewards. I suggest you pick a theme—either choose a specific celebration or just have a general French theme like "Parisian Sidewalk Cafe." Select appropriate music and ask your guests to dress for the occasion.

Buy French wine and make some French food to observe the occasion. Choose any recipes you like or try your hand at this one—my grandmother Louise's simple and delicious recipe for onion soup. My mother, Roselyne, gave it to me.

QUICK ⬛ *PAINLESS*

Printemps also is the name of a popular Parisian department store.

IF YOU'RE SO
INCLINED

Never plan to go shopping on Sunday in Europe—nearly everything is closed. Do your shopping during the week.

La Soupe à l'Oignon de Mémé Louise *(Serves 4)*

One large onion, sliced

2 tablespoons butter

1 tablespoon flour

4 cups water

Salt to taste

Freshly ground black pepper to taste

4 slices country bread

1 cup *gruyère*, grated

1 In a large saucepan, heat the butter over a very low flame until melted. Add the onion and sautè until it becomes translucent (about 20 minutes). Sprinkle in the flour and stir to combine.

2 Add the water, little by little, stirring as you go. Add salt and pepper to taste. Turn the heat up to medium and cook for 20 to 25 minutes.

3 As the soup cooks, toast the slices of bread. (My mother does this in the broiler because French bread is very thick and won't fit in the toaster.)

4 Preheat the oven to 300 degrees.

5 Put one piece of bread in each serving bowl. Divide the soup between the four bowls. Sprinkle each with the grated *gruyère* and then put the bowls in the oven for 10 minutes to melt the cheese.

6 Serve immediately with a green salad and white wine.

More Lazy Stuff

How to Get Someone Else to Do It

Other people can't learn French for you, but they certainly can assist you. The following are some suggestions for how to use others to your advantage.

TUTOR

The most expensive way to ease the pain of learning French is to engage a personal tutor. Some people find one-on-one teaching sessions to be a very effective supplement to text learning. This choice is hard on the budget, but if money is no object, you can find a personal tutor by inquiring at the sources listed for classes in the following section.

CLASSES

Although this book strives to avoid traditional textbook learning, perhaps you'll want to continue your study of French beyond the scope of this book. If so, you'll probably find that many helpful classes are offered in your area. A complete listing of available courses would be too lengthy to include here. Instead, I'll just point out some of the institutions in your area that offer French classes. Note that some institutions offer short term instruction, while others teach classes that last for several years.

Local university or community college

Alliance Française

Berlitz (an expensive choice—ideal for business learners)

MEDIA

Nothing is a better substitute for traveling to France than immersing your-self in French media. You can use your own mixture of audio tapes, com-pact discs, and movies to keep you surrounded by the delightful roar of the French "r". Here's a listing of some audio tapes. You can listen to them during your morning commute or can even play them while you sleep!

Audio tapes:

Colette (Well-Spoken Companion Series) by Colette (The Audio Partners Publishing Corporation, 1997).

French (book & cassette) by Richard Caudle (Rock 'N Learn, 1994).

A L'Aventure: Beginning French by Anne C. Cummings (John Wiley & Sons, 1996).

Rhyme Time: A Beginner's Collection of Nursery Rhymes Translated into French by Marilyn Simundson-Olson (Global Rhyme Time, Inc., 1996).

Teach Me French: A Musical Journey Through the Day (Teach Me Tapes, 1996).

Teach Yourself Instant French by Elizabeth Smith (Ntc Pub Audio, 1999).

Voilà! A New Course in French for Adult Beginners by Jacqueline Gonthier (Barrons Educational Audio, 1997).

French: A Complete Course for Beginners by Gaelle Graham (Teach Yourself, 1993).

French (set of six) (Oasis Audio, 1989).

Talk French (Ntc Pub Audio, 1999).

Suggestions for French movies and music can be found in Chapter 3, and Chapter 5, respectively.

If You Really Want More, Read These

ENGLISH LANGUAGE

For atmosphere:

Hemingway, Ernest. *A Moveable Feast*. New York. Touchstone Books, 1996.

Kaplan, Alice. *French Lessons*. Chicago. University of Chicago Press, 1993.

Liebeling, A.J. *Between Meals: An Appetite for Paris*. New York. North Point Press, 1986.

Mayle, Peter. *A Year in Provence*. New York. Vintage Books, 1991.

Pagnol, Marcel. *My Father's Glory* and *My Mother's Castle*. (in translation) New York. North Point Press, 1986.

For food:

Marshall, Lydie. *A Passion for My Provence: Cooking From the South of France*. New York. HarperCollins, 1995.

Olney, Richard. *Simple French Food*. New York. Macmillan General Reference, 1992.

Wells, Patricia. *Bistro Cooking*. New York. Workman Publishing Company, 1989.

Young, Daniel. *The Paris Cafe Cookbook: Rendezvous & Recipes from 50 Best Cafes*. New York. William Morrow & Company, 1998.

For language and culture:

Platt, Polly. *French or Foe?* New York. Distribooks, 1998.

Stein, Gail. *The Complete Idiot's Guide to Learning French On Your Own,* Second Edition. New York. Macmillan General Reference, 1999.

For fun:

Tom, Howard. *Wicked French*. New York. Workman Publishing Company, 1989.

Guidebooks:

Couch, Gordon. *Access in Paris: A Guide for Those Who Have Problems Getting Around*. New York. Cimino Publishing Group, 1994.

Gershman, Suzy. *Frommer's Born to Shop Paris*. New York. Macmillan General Reference, 1997.

Wells, Patricia. *The Food Lover's Guide to France*. New York. Workman Publishing Company, 1987.

Wells, Patricia. *The Food Lover's Guide to Paris*. New York. Workman Publishing Company, 1999.

Wurman, Richard Saul. *Paris Access*. New York. Access Press, 1996.

FRENCH LANGUAGE

De Saint-Exupery, Antoine. *Le Petit Prince*. New York. Harcourt Brace, 1969.

Goscinny and Uderzo. The *Asterix* series (extremely complex French with many idioms and much word play, but worth the trouble). Dargaud Editeur, 12 rue Blaise-Pascal 92201 Neuilly-sur-Seine, Paris.

Hergé. The *Tintin* series. Casterman, Belgium.

Sempe, J. *Le Petit Nicolas*. New York. Schoenhof's Foreign Books, 1989.

WEB SITES

French books:

www.amazon.com

www.dawson.co.uk

www.lingua.co.uk

www.transglobalbooks.com

www.europa-pages.co.uk

www.mantrapublishing.com

www.celf.fr

www.comitis.com

www.bookswithoutborders.com

French culture:

www.franceandus.com

www.france.com

www.traveldocs.com/fr

If You Don't Know
What It Means, Look Here

A

à   at; to

à l'étranger   abroad

abricot (m)   apricot

absolument   absolutely

absurde   absurd

abuser de   abuse, to

accident (m)   accident

accompagner   accompany, to

acheter   buy, to

acteur (m)   actor

admirer   admire, to

adresse (f)   address

adulte (n)   adult

aéroport (m)   airport

affaire (f)   business

âge (m)   age

agence (f)   agency

agent (m) de police   police officer

agents (m, pl) de conservation   preservatives

agneau (m)   lamb

agréable   nice

aider   assist, to; help, to

ail (m)   garlic

aimer   enjoy oneself, to like

aimer beaucoup   love, to

air (m)   air

ajouter   add, to

alimentation (f)   diet

aller   go, to

aller et retour (m) round-trip ticket

allumette (f) match

alors then

ambitieux ambitious

américain American

ami (m) friend

amour (m) love

an (m) year

ancien old; ancient

animal (m) animal

animal (m) familier pet

anniversaire (m) anniversary; birthday

annonce (f) announcement

annuler cancel, to

août August

appareil-photo (m) camera

appartement (m) apartment

appeler call, to

apporter bring, to

apprendre learn, to

après after

après-midi afternoon

aquarium (m) aquarium

arbre (m) tree

arc-en-ciel (m) rainbow

arche (f) arch

architecture (f) architecture

argent (m) cash; money

arrêter stop

arriver arrive, to

art (m) art

artichaut (m) artichoke

article (m) article

artiste (n) artist

ascenseur (m) elevator

aspirine (f) aspirin

assez enough

assiette (f) plate

assurance (f) insurance

assuré safe (sure)

atmosphère (f) atmosphere

attendre wait, to

attirer attract, to

au-dessus de above

au lieu instead

au revoir goodbye

Au secours! Help!

au sujet de about

aubergine (f) eggplant

aujourd'hui (m) today

aussi also

automne autumn

autour around

autre other

avant before

avare stingy

avec with

avion (m) airplane

avoir have, to

avoir besoin de need, to

avril April

B

bagages (m, pl) luggage

baiser kiss, to

balader stroll, to

balcon (m) balcony

banane (f) banana

bandage (m) bandage

banque (f) bank

barbe (f) beard

bateau (m) ship

batterie (f) battery

beau beautiful; handsome

beau-frère (m) brother-in-law

beau-père (m) father-in-law

beaucoup much

bébé (m) baby

bête stupid

bibliothèque (f) library

bicyclette (f) bicycle

bien well

bien sûr of course

bientôt soon

bière (f) beer

bifteck (m) steak

bijoutier (m) jewelry store

billet (m) ticket

billion (m) billion

bizarre strange

blanc white

blé (m) corn

bleu blue

blond blond

bœuf (m) beef

boire drink, to

bon good

bon marché bargain

Bon voyage! Have a good trip!

bonne (f) maid

botte (f) boot

bouche (f) mouth

boucher (m) butcher

bouillir boil, to

boulanger (m) bakery

bourdon (m) bumblebee

bouteille (f) bottle

boutique (f) shop

bras (m) arm

brosse à dents (f) toothbrush

brouillard (m) fog

bruit (m) noise

brun brown

bureau (m) office

bus (m) bus

C

ça va How is it going?

cable (m) cable television

cacher hide, to

cadeau (m) gift

café (m) coffee

café (m) au lait coffee with milk

caissier (m) cashier

calculer calculate, to

calmar (m) squid

calme calm

camping (m) camping

canadien Canadian

canard (m) duck

carnet (m) notebook

carte (f) map

carte (f) de crédit credit card

carte postale (f) postcard

casser break, to

cathédrale (f) cathedral

catholique Catholic

ce, cet, cette this; that

ceinture (f) belt

célèbre famous

célébrer celebrate, to

célibataire single

cendrier (m) ashtray

centre center

cerise (f) cherry

chair (f) flesh

chaise (f) chair

chaleur (f) heat

chambre (f) bedroom

champ (m) field

champignon (m) mushroom

changer change, to

chanson (f) song

chanter sing, to

chapeau (m) hat

chaque each

charcuterie (m) meat shop

chat (m) cat

châtain brunette

château-fort (m) castle

chaud hot

chaussure (f) shoe

chef-d'œvre (m) masterpiece

chemin (m) path

chemise (f) shirt

cher dear; expensive

chercher search, to

cheval (m) horse

cheveux (m, pl) hair

chez at the home of

chien (m) dog

chinois Chinese

chocolat (m) chocolate

choisir choose, to

chose (f) thing

chrétien Christian

ciel (m) sky

cigarette (f) cigarette

cinéma (m) cinema

cinq five

cité (f) city

citoyen (m) citizen

citron (m) lemon

clair clear

classe (f) class

classique classical

cléf (f) key

client (m) customer

climat (m) climate

climatisation (f) air conditioning

cœur (f) heart

coiffeur (m) barber; hairdresser

combien how much

commander order, to

comme as

commencer begin, to

comment how

communiquer communicate, to

complet booked (fully)

complètement completely

comprendre understand, to

compris included (cost)

compte (m) bill; check

compter count, to

concert (m) concert

conclure conclude, to

condition (f) condition

conduire drive, to

connaître know, to (someone)

construction (f) building

contenter satisfy, to

contre against

corps (m) body

correspondre correspond, to

costume (m) suit

côte (f) coast

coton (m) cotton

cou (m) neck

coudre sew, to

couleur (f) color

courageux courageous

courses automobiles (f, pl)
auto racing

court short

cousin (m) cousin

couteau (m) knife

coûter cost, to

couvert cloudy

couverture (f) blanket

cracher spit, to

crainte (f) fear

crayon (m) pencil

créer create, to

crème (f) cream

crémerie (f) dairy store

crevette grise (n) shrimp

crier cry, to

croire believe, to

croisière (f) cruise

croquis (m) sketch

cuiller (f) spoon

cuir (m) leather

cuire cook, to

cuisine (f) kitchen; cooking

culotte (f) pants

culture (f) culture

curieux curious

curiosité (f) curiosity

D

d'abord   first (before)

dangereux   dangerous

dans   in

danser   dance, to

de   of; from; about

de nouveau   again

de plus   besides

de rien   you're welcome

décembre   December

décider   decide, to

dedans   inside

défense de fumer   no smoking

degré (m)   degree

dehors   outside

déjà   already

déjeuner (m)   lunch

délicieux   delicious

demain (m)   tomorrow

demander   ask, to

demi (m)   half

dent (m)   tooth

dentelle (f)   lace

dentifrice (m)   toothpaste

dentiste (n)   dentist

départ (m)   departure

dépense (f)   expense

dépenser   spend, to

dernier   last

derrière   behind

descendre   descend, to

désirer   desire, to

destination (f)   destination

déterminer   determine, to

détester   hate, to

deux   two

devoir   must (to have to)

d'habitude   usually

diabétique   diabetic

dieu (m)   god

difficile   difficult

dimanche   Sunday

dîner (m)   dinner

dire   say, to

directeur (m)   manager

discothèque (m)   disco

discussion (f)   discussion

discuter   discuss, to

disponible   available

divorcé   divorced

dix   ten

dix-huit   eighteen

dix-neuf   nineteen

dix-sept   seventeen

docteur (m)   doctor

doigt (m)   finger

dollar (m)   dollar

donner   give, to

dormir   sleep, to

dos (m)   back

douane (f)   customs

double   double

douche (f) shower

douleur (f) pain

doux soft

douze twelve

droit right

drôle funny

E

eau (f) water

échanger exchange, to

écharpe (f) scarf

èclair (m) lightning

école (f) school

écrire write, to

église (f) church

élégant elegant

élévateur (m) elevator

employé (m) employee

employer use, to

en some

en bas downstairs

en colère angry

en effet indeed

en haut upstairs

en retard late

encore yet

enfant (n) child

enfin finally

ennemi (m) enemy

ensemble together

entre between

entrée (f) entrance

entrer enter, to

enveloppe (f) envelope

environ approximately

envoyer send, to

épouser marry, to

époux (m) spouse

erreur (f) mistake

escalier (m) staircase

escargot (m) snail

espagnol Spanish

espérer hope, to

essayer try (on), to

essence (f) gasoline

est (m) east

estomac (m) stomach

et and

été (m) summer

étranger (m) foreigner; stranger

être be, to

étudiant (m) student

étudier study, to

exactement exactly

excellent excellent

excursion (f) excursion

excuser excuse, to

expérience (f) experience

expliquer explain, to

expression (f) expression; phrase

F

fabuleux fabulous

facile easy

faible weak

faim (f) hunger

faire do, to; make, to

faire marcher operate, to

fait (m) fact

famille (f) family

fantastique fantastic; stupendous

fatigué tired

faux wrong; false

femme (f) wife; woman

fenêtre (f) window

ferme firm

fermé closed

ferme (f) farm

fermer close, to

fête (f) party

feu (m) fire

feuille (f) leaf

feuille (f) de papier sheet of paper

février February

fiancé (m) fiance

fier proud

fille (f) daughter; girl

film (m) movie

fils (m) son; boy

fin (f) end

finir finish, to

fleur (f) flower

foie (m) liver

fonctionner function, to

fondre melt, to

fontaine (f) fountain

football (m) soccer

football américain (m) football

forêt (f) forest

fort strong

fourchette (f) fork

frais cool

français French

frère (m) brother

frites (f, pl) French fries

froid cold

fromage (m) cheese

fruit (m) fruit

fumer smoke, to

G

gagner win, to

gant (m) glove

garage (m) garage

garçon (m) boy

gare (f) railroad station

gâteau (m) cake

gauche left

gencive (f) gum

généreux generous

genoux (m, pl) knees

genre (m) type (kind)

gens (m, pl) people

gentil nice

glace (f) ice; ice cream

gorge (f) throat

goûter   taste, to
gramme (m)   gram
grand   big; tall
grand-mère (f)   grandmother
grand-père (m)   grandfather
grand lit (m)   bed (queen)
grand magasin (m)   store
grand'route (f)   highway
gravir   ascend, to
grec   Greek
grenier (m)   attic
gronder   scold, to
gros   fat
groupe (m)   group
guerre (f)   war
guichet (m)   counter (window)
guitare (f)   guitar
gymnase (m)   gym

H

habiter   reside, to
haricot (m)   bean
hauteur (f)   haughtiness
heure (f)   hour; time
heureux   happy; lucky
hier   yesterday
homme (m)   man
honnête   honest
hôpital (m)   hospital
horloge (f)   clock
horreur (f)   horror
horrible   horrible

hors d'œuvre (m)   appetizer
hôtel (m)   hotel
huile (f)   oil
huile (f) solaire   suntan oil
huit   eight
humble   humble
humide   humid

I

ici   here
idée (f)   idea
idiot (m)   idiot
il y a   there is
île (f)   island
illuminer   light/turn on, to
immédiatement   immediately
impoli   rude
important   important
indiquer   indicate, to
infinitif (m)   infinitive
infirmière (f)   nurse
information (f)   information
informer   inform, to
ingénieux   clever
intelligent   intelligent
intense   intense
intéressant   interesting
interroger   question, to
inviter   invite, to
italien   Italian
ivre   drunk

J

jaloux jealous

jamais ever; never

jambe (f) leg

janvier January

japonais Japanese

jardin (m) garden

jaune yellow

Je m'excuse I'm sorry

jeudi Thursday

jeune young

joli pretty

jouer play, to

jouer aux cartes play cards, to

jour (m) day

journal (m) newspaper

juif Jewish

juillet July

juin June

jupe (f) skirt

juriste (m) lawyer

K

kascher kosher

kilogramme (m) kilogram

L

là there

lac (m) lake

laid ugly

laine (f) wool

lait (m) milk

langue (f) language

laver wash, to

laverie (f) laundry service

le, la, les the

leçon (f) lesson

légume (m) vegetable

lent slow

lentement slowly

lettre (f) letter

lever raise, to

librairie (n) bookshop

lieu (m) place

ligne (f) line

lire read, to

liste (f) list

lit (m) bed

lit (m) à une place bed (single)

lit (m) double bed (double)

litre (n) liter

livre (m) book

local local

loin far

long long

louer hire, to; rent, to

lourd heavy

lumière (f) light

lundi Monday

lune (f) moon

lunettes (f, pl) eye glasses

lycée (m) highschool

M

Madame Mrs., Ms.

Mademoiselle Miss

magasin (m) shop

magazine (m) magazine

mai May

maillot (m) bathing suit

main (f) hand

maintenant now

mais but

maison (f) house

malsain unhealthy

manger eat, to

manquer miss, to

manteau (m) coat

marché (m) market

marcher walk, to

mardi Tuesday

mari (m) husband

marié married

mars March

mathématiques (f, pl) mathematics

matin (m) morning

mauvais bad

mécanicien (m) mechanic

méchant mean; nasty

mécontenter displeasing

médecine (f) medicine

médicament (m) drug

meilleur better

mer (f) sea

merci beaucoup thank you

mercredi Wednesday

mère (f) mother

merveilleux marvelous

mesure (f) measure, size

métro (m) subway

mettre put, to

midi (m) noon

mignon cute

mince thin

minuit (m) midnight

minute (f) minute

miroir (m) mirror

moderne modern

moins less

moins … que less than

mois (m) month

moitié (f) half

moment (m) moment

Mon Dieu! My God!

Monsieur Mr., sir

montagne (f) mountain

morceau (m) piece

mot (m) word

moteur (m) motor

mouchoir (m) tissue

mourir die, to

mouton (m) sheep

musée (m) museum

musique (f) music

N

nager swim, to

naissance (f) birth

naître be born, to

nation (f) nation

naturel naturel

navette (f) airport shuttle bus

ne ... jamais never

ne ... pas not

ne ... personne nobody

ne ... plus no longer

ne ... rien nothing

nécessaire necessary

négociant (m) merchant

neige (f) snow

nerveux nervous

nettoyer clean, to

neuf nine

neveu (m) nephew

nez (m) nose

nièce (f) niece

Noël Christmas

noir black

nom (m) name; noun

nom (m) de famille last name; surname

nombre (m) number

nomination (f) appointment

non no

nord (m) north

normal normal

nourrisson (m) infant

nouveau new

nouvelle (f) news

novembre November

nuage (m) cloud

nuit (f) night

O

obscur dark

observer watch

océan (m) ocean

octobre October

odeur (f) odor

œil (m) eye

œuf (m) egg

offenser offend, to

officiel official

offrir offer, to

oie (f) goose

oignon (m) onion

oiseau (m) bird

olive (f) olive

ombre (f) shadow

on (pronoun) one

oncle (m) uncle

onze eleven

opéra (m) opera

or (m) gold

orage (m) storm

orange orange

oreille (f) ear

oreiller (m) pillow

original original

ou or

où where

oublier forget, to

ouest (m) west

oui yes

ouvert open

P

pain (m) bread

paire (f) pair

pamplemousse (m) grapefruit

pansement (m) adhésif Band-Aid

pantalons (m, pl) pants

papetier (m) stationary store

papier (m) paper

papier (m) hygiénique toilet paper

Pâques (f, pl) Easter

paquet (m) package

paradis (m) paradise

parapluie (m) umbrella

parc (m) park

parce que because

parcours (m) golf course

pardessus (m) overcoat

parent (m) relative

paresseux lazy

parfait perfect

parfum (m) perfume

parking (m) parking lot

parler speak, to

Parlez-vous anglais? Do you speak English?

partir depart, to

partout everywhere

pas not

passé out of style

passé composé past tense

passeport (m) passport

passer pass, to

pâte (f) pastry

pâtes (f, pl) pasta

patron (m) boss

pauvre poor

payer pay, to

pays (m) country

peau (f) skin

peigner comb, to

peindre paint, to

peinture (f) painting

pendant while

penser think, to

perdre lose, to

père (m) father

personne (f) person

peser weigh, to

petit little; small

petit-fils (m) grandson

petit ami (m) boyfriend

petit déjeuner (m) breakfast

petite-fille (f) granddaughter

peu (m) little bit

peut-être maybe

phare (m) headlight

pharmacie (f) pharmacy

pièce (f) room

pièce de monnaie (f) coin

pied (m) foot

pique-nique (m) picnic

piscine (f) pool

place (f) square (plaza)

plage (f) beach

plaire à please, to

plaisant pleasing

plat (m) course

plein full

pleuvoir rain, to

pluc (m) nerd

pluie (f) rain

plus ... que more than

pneu (m) tire

pneu (m) crevé flat tire

poche (f) pocket

poisson (m) fish

poivre (m) pepper

poli courteous

politique (f, pl) politics

pomme (f) apple

pomme (f) de terre potato

porc (m) pork

porte-monnaie (m) purse

porte (f) door

portefeuille (m) wallet

porter carry, to

portier (m) doorman

possibilité (f) possibility

possible possible

poste (f) mail; post office

poulet (m) chicken

pour for (in order to)

pourcentage (m) percentage

pourquoi why

pouvoir can (to be able)

premier first

prendre take, to

préparer prepare, to

près near

prescription (f) prescription

présenter present, to

préservatif (m) condom

prêt ready

prêt à porter ready to wear

printemps (m) spring

privé private

prix (m) price

probabilité (f) probability

problème (m) problem

professeur (m) professor; teacher

profession (f) profession

programme (m) schedule

prononcer pronounce, to

propre clean

propriétaire (n) owner

protéger protect, to

puces (f, pl) flea markets

Q

quand when

quart four

quatorze fourteen

quel which

qui who, whom

quinze fifteen

quitter leave (something), to

quoi what

R

race (f) race

raconter tell, to

radiateur (m) radiator

raisin (m) grape

rapide rapid

rappeler call back, to

recette (f) recipe

recevoir receive, to

recommander recommend, to

regarder look, to

région (f) region

relâcher relax, to

relation (f) connection

religion (f) religion

remise (f) discount

rencontrer meet, to

réparer repair, to

repas (m) meal

répéter repeat, to

répondre respond, to

réponse (f) answer

représenter represent, to

réservation (f) reservation

réserver reserve, to

résoudre resolve, to

respecter respect, to

respirer breathe, to

restaurant (m) restaurant

rester stay, to

retraite (f) pension

réveille-matin (m) alarm clock

revenir return, to

rêver dream, to

rhume (m) cold (sick)

riche rich

ridicule ridiculous

rire laugh, to

rivière (f) river

riz (m) rice

robe (f) dress

romantique romantic

rose pink; rose

rouge red

rue (f) street

S

sac (m) bag

sage wise

saint (m) saint

saison (f) season

salade (f) salad

salaire (m) salary

sale dirty

salle (f) de bains bathroom

salle à manger (f) dining room

salon (m) living room

salon (m) d'essayage dressing room

samedi Saturday

sandale (f) sandal

sans without

santé (f) health

s'attendre à anticipate, to

savoir know, to (something)

savon (m) soap

se baigner bathe, to

se coucher go to bed, to

se dépêcher hurry, to

se déplacer move, to

se lever get up, to

se passer happen, to

se rappeler remember, to

se réveiller wake up, to

se tromper err, to

sèche-cheveux (m) hairdryer

sécher dry, to

seconde (f) second

secrétaire (n) secretary

seize sixteen

sel (m) salt

semaine (f) week

sensible sensitive

sept seven

septembre September

sérieux serious

serrer hug, to

serveur (m) waiter

service (m) service

services (m, pl) en chambres room service

serviette (f) napkin; towel

serviettes (f, pl) hygiéniques sanitary pads

servir serve, to

seul alone

seulement only

s'éveiller awaken, to

s'habiller dress, to

shampooing (m) shampoo

si if

siècle (m) century

siege (m) seat

signe (m) sign

s'il vous plaît please

simple simple

sincère sincere

six six

snob (m) snob

sœur (f) sister

soie (f) silk

soif (f) thirst

soir (m) evening

soireé **(f)** party

soleil **(m)** sun

sommelier **(m)** wine steward

sortie **(f)** exit

soupe **(f)** soup

sourire smile, to

souris **(f)** mouse

sous beneath

sous-sol **(m)** basement

sous-vêtements **(m, pl)** underwear

soutien-gorge **(m)** bra

souvent often

spécial special

splendide splendid

stade **(m)** stadium

station-service **(f)** gas station

stylo **(m)** pen

sucre **(m)** sugar

sucre candi **(m)** candy

sud **(m)** south

suivre follow, to

superbe magnificent

supermarché **(m)** supermarket

supplémentaire extra

supposer imagine, to

sur on top of; on; up

symbole **(m)** symbol

T

tabac **(m)** tobacco shop

table **(f)** table

taille **(f)** size

tante **(f)** aunt

tasse **(f)** cup

taxe **(f)** tax

teinturerie **(f)** dry cleaner

téléphone **(m)** telephone

télévision **(f)** television

température **(f)** temperature

temps **(m)** weather

tendu tight

terrasse **(f)** terrace

terre **(f)** earth, dirt

tête **(f)** head

thé **(m)** tea

théâtre **(m)** theater

timbre **(m)** postage stamp

toile **(f)** cloth

toilettes **(f, pl)** toilet

toit **(m)** roof

tomate **(f)** tomato

tomber fall, to

tomber en panne breakdown

tôt early

total **(m)** total

toucher touch, to

toujours always

touriste **(n)** tourist

tout entirely

train **(m)** train

traivailler work, to

transport **(m)** transportation

transporter fly, to
treize thirteen
très very
tricot (m) sweater
triste sad
trois three
trop too (much)
tropical tropical
trouver find, to
truc (m) way; device
tuer kill, to

U
un one
usine (f) factory

V
vacances (f, pl) vacation
vache (f) cow
valise (f) suitcase
végétarian vegetarian
vélo (m) bicycling
vendre sell, to
vendredi Friday
venir come, to
vent (m) wind
vente (f) sale
vérifier check, to
verre (m) glass
vert green
veste (f) jacket
vêtements (m, pl) clothing

veuve (f) widow
viande (f) meat
vide empty
vieux old
ville (f) town
vin (m) wine
vin (m) mousseux sparkling wine
vinaigre (m) vinegar
vingt twenty
violence (f) violence
violet purple
visage (m) face
visiter visit, to
vite quickly
vivre live, to
voir see, to
voisin next
voiture (f) car
voiture de location (f) rental car
voler steal, to
voter vote, to
vouloir want, to
voyage (m) tour; trip
voyager travel, to
vrai true, real
vue (f) view

Y–Z
yeux (m, pl) eyes
Zut alors! Oh, rats!

D

It's Time for Your Reward

Congratulations. You have mastered French the Lazy Way. You deserve a reward for all your efforts.

Once You've Done This ...	Reward Yourself with This ...
Learned the French alphabet	Sing your A-B-Cs
Learned how to count in French	Take a nap and count sheep in French
Learned how to make your own cognates	Translate useful English terms into their French counterparts
Conjugated a few verbs	Enjoy some action—walk around your neighborhood, talk to friends, or just relax
Learned how to address people	Start calling your family by their French names (Madame, Monsieur, and so on)
Learned the art of pleasant conversation	Call a fellow French student for a chat
Learned some French food terms	Cook yourself a nice dinner and open a bottle of wine and toast yourself

Once You've Done This ...	Reward Yourself with This ...
Learned how to order a French meal	Take yourself out for a nice bite
Learned some French shopping terms	Hit the boutiques and lighten your wallet
Learned French travel terms	Book a trip to France (or Montreal)
Become familiar with French culture	Go to a museum and look at French art
Learned how to solve problems in France	Relax and know that you'll be prepared for unexpected events
Learned how the French celebrate	Plan a Bastille Day party

Where to Find What You're Looking For

Now you can do these tasks, too!

The Lazy Way

Starting to think there are a few more of life's little tasks that you've been putting off? Don't worry—we've got you covered. Take a look at all of *The Lazy Way* books available. Just imagine—you can do almost anything *The Lazy Way!*

Handle Your Money The Lazy Way
By Sarah Young Fisher and Carol Turkington
0-02-862632-X

Build Your Financial Future The Lazy Way
By Terry Meany
0-02-862648-6

Cut Your Spending The Lazy Way
By Leslie Haggin
0-02-863002-5

Have Fun with Your Kids The Lazy Way
By Marilee Lebon
0-02-863166-8

Keep Your Kids Busy The Lazy Way
By Barbara Nielsen and Patrick Wallace
0-02-863013-0

Feed Your Kids Right The Lazy Way
By Virginia Van Vynckt
0-02-863001-7

*All Lazy Way books are just $12.95!

additional titles on the back!

Learn French The Lazy Way
By Christophe Desmaison
0-02-863011-4

Learn German The Lazy Way
By Amy Kardel
0-02-863165-X

Learn Spanish The Lazy Way
By Steven R. Hawson
0-02-862650-8

Redecorate Your Home The Lazy Way
By Rebecca Jerdee
0-02-863163-3

Shed Some Pounds The Lazy Way
By Annette Cain and Becky Cortopassi-
Carlson
0-02-862999-X

Shop Online The Lazy Way
By Richard Seltzer
0-02-863173-0

Clean Your House The Lazy Way
By Barbara H. Durham
0-02-862649-4

Care for Your Home The Lazy Way
By Terry Meany
0-02-862646-X

Stop Aging The Lazy Way
By Judy Myers, Ph.D.
0-02-862793-8

Get in Shape The Lazy Way
By Annette Cain
0-02-863010-6

Learn to Sew The Lazy Way
By Lydia Wills
0-02-863167-6

Train Your Dog The Lazy Way
By Andrea Arden
0-87605180-8

Organize Your Stuff The Lazy Way
By Toni Ahlgren
0-02-863000-9

Manage Your Time The Lazy Way
By Toni Ahlgren
0-02-863169-2

Take Care of Your Car The Lazy Way
By Michael Kennedy and Carol
Turkington
0-02-862647-8

Get a Better Job The Lazy Way
By Susan Ireland
0-02-863399-7

Cook Your Meals The Lazy Way
By Sharon Bowers
0-02-862644-3

Cooking Vegetarian The Lazy Way
By Barbara Grunes
0-02-863158-7

Master the Grill The Lazy Way
By Pamela Rice Hahn and Keith
Giddeon
0-02-863157-9